Spring into Mental Maths with CGP!

The daffodils are out, lambs are in the fields, the days are getting longer... it must be time for some Mental Maths Daily Practice from CGP!

This brilliant book covers a huge range of skills from the Year 6 curriculum, with a page of practice for every day of the spring term.

And it doesn't stop there — this treasure trove of examples and colourful pictures will keep pupils engaged in class and at home. Spring-tastic!

What CGP is all about

Our sole aim here at CGP is to produce the highest quality books — carefully written, immaculately presented and dangerously close to being funny.

Then we work our socks off to get them out to you — at the cheapest possible prices.

Contents

☑ Use the tick boxes to help keep a record of which tests have been attempted.

Week 1
- ☑ Day 1 1
- ☑ Day 2 2
- ☑ Day 3 3
- ☑ Day 4 4
- ☑ Day 5 5

Week 2
- ☑ Day 1 6
- ☑ Day 2 7
- ☑ Day 3 8
- ☑ Day 4 9
- ☑ Day 5 10

Week 3
- ☑ Day 1 11
- ☑ Day 2 12
- ☑ Day 3 13
- ☑ Day 4 14
- ☑ Day 5 15

Week 4
- ☑ Day 1 16
- ☑ Day 2 17
- ☑ Day 3 18
- ☑ Day 4 19
- ☑ Day 5 20

Week 5
- ☑ Day 1 21
- ☑ Day 2 22
- ☑ Day 3 23
- ☑ Day 4 24
- ☑ Day 5 25

Week 6
- ☑ Day 1 26
- ☑ Day 2 27
- ☑ Day 3 28
- ☑ Day 4 29
- ☑ Day 5 30

Week 7
- ☑ Day 1 31
- ☑ Day 2 32
- ☑ Day 3 33
- ☑ Day 4 34
- ☑ Day 5 35

Week 8
- ☑ Day 1 36
- ☑ Day 2 37
- ☑ Day 3 38
- ☑ Day 4 39
- ☑ Day 5 40

Week 9
- [ ] Day 1 41
- [ ] Day 2 42
- [ ] Day 3 43
- [ ] Day 4 44
- [ ] Day 5 45

Week 10
- [ ] Day 1 46
- [ ] Day 2 47
- [ ] Day 3 48
- [ ] Day 4 49
- [ ] Day 5 50

Week 11
- [ ] Day 1 51
- [ ] Day 2 52
- [ ] Day 3 53
- [ ] Day 4 54
- [ ] Day 5 55

Week 12
- [ ] Day 1 56
- [ ] Day 2 57
- [ ] Day 3 58
- [ ] Day 4 59
- [ ] Day 5 60

Answers 61

Published by CGP

ISBN: 978 1 78908 776 5

Editors: Katherine Faudemer, Katie Fernandez, Emily Forsberg, Tamara Sinivassen and George Wright

With thanks to Alison Griffin and Glenn Rogers for the proofreading.

With thanks to Lottie Edwards for the copyright research.

Clipart from Corel®

Printed by Elanders Ltd, Newcastle upon Tyne.
Based on the classic CGP style created by Richard Parsons.

Text, design, layout and original illustrations © Coordination Group Publications Ltd. (CGP) 2021
All rights reserved.

Photocopying this book is not permitted, even if you have a CLA licence.
Extra copies are available from CGP with next day delivery • 0800 1712 712 • www.cgpbooks.co.uk

How to Use this Book

- This book contains 60 daily practice tests.
- We've split them into 12 sections — that's roughly one for each week of the Year 6 spring term.
- Each week is made up of 5 tests, so there's one for every school day of the term (Monday – Friday).
- Each test should take about 10 minutes to complete.
- Pupils should aim to do their working in their heads, without writing anything down.
- The tests contain a mix of Mental Maths topics from Year 6. New Year 6 topics are gradually introduced as you go through the book.
- The tests increase in difficulty as you progress through the term.
- Each test looks something like this:

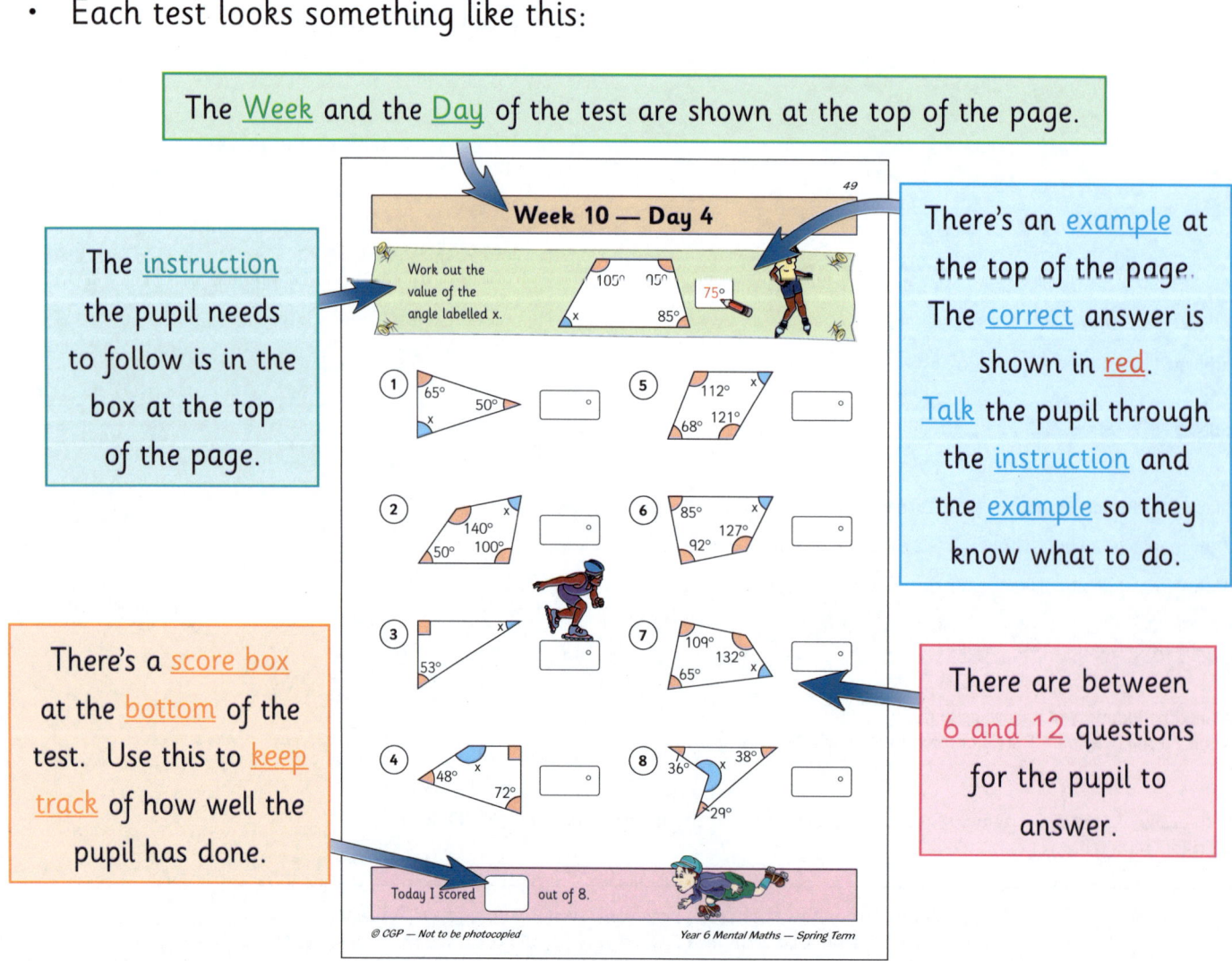

Week 1 — Day 1

Circle the prime number. 75 (73) 57

1) 10 5 25

2) 42 37 38

3) 2 9 15

4) 25 11 1

5) 35 21 7

6) 27 23 33

7) 63 61 69

8) 67 66 77

9) 99 97 93

10) 49 39 29

11) 53 51 55

12) 83 87 81

Today I scored ☐ out of 12.

Week 1 — Day 2

Write the answer to the calculation as a mixed number. $6\frac{3}{4} - 4\frac{1}{2} = \boxed{2\frac{1}{4}}$

1) $1\frac{1}{6} + 2\frac{2}{3} = \boxed{}$

2) $3\frac{1}{5} + 4\frac{7}{10} = \boxed{}$

3) $4\frac{7}{8} - 1\frac{1}{4} = \boxed{}$

4) $5\frac{3}{4} + 2\frac{1}{8} = \boxed{}$

5) $2\frac{5}{9} + 6\frac{1}{3} = \boxed{}$

6) $8\frac{1}{2} - 3\frac{1}{8} = \boxed{}$

7) $6\frac{1}{2} - 5\frac{2}{10} = \boxed{}$

8) $3\frac{2}{3} + 6\frac{3}{12} = \boxed{}$

9) $7\frac{8}{12} - 4\frac{1}{4} = \boxed{}$

10) $4\frac{5}{15} + 3\frac{2}{5} = \boxed{}$

11) $9\frac{19}{20} - 7\frac{3}{5} = \boxed{}$

12) $2\frac{1}{2} + 5\frac{7}{12} = \boxed{}$

Today I scored ☐ out of 12.

Week 1 — Day 3

The difference between the height above sea level of a bridge and a tunnel is shown. Work out the missing height.

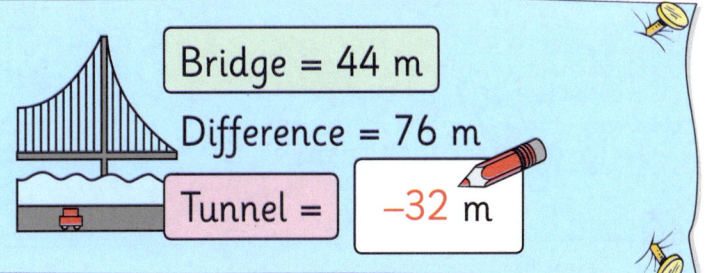
Bridge = 44 m
Difference = 76 m
Tunnel = −32 m

1.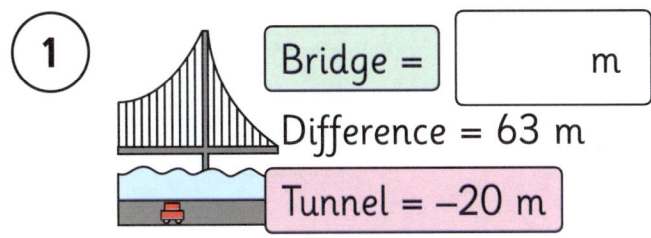
Bridge = ___ m
Difference = 63 m
Tunnel = −20 m

2.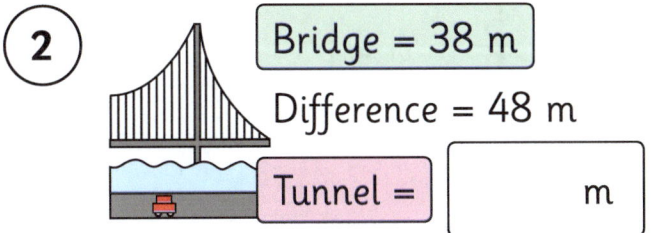
Bridge = 38 m
Difference = 48 m
Tunnel = ___ m

3.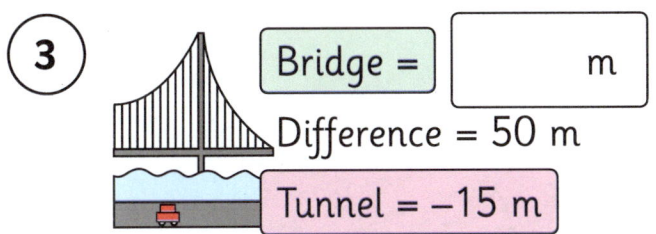
Bridge = ___ m
Difference = 50 m
Tunnel = −15 m

4.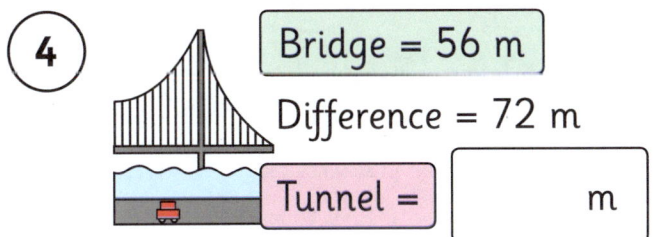
Bridge = 56 m
Difference = 72 m
Tunnel = ___ m

5.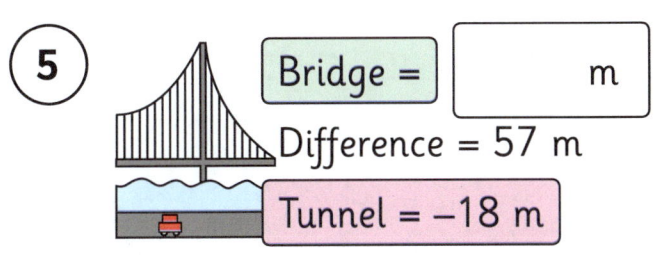
Bridge = ___ m
Difference = 57 m
Tunnel = −18 m

6.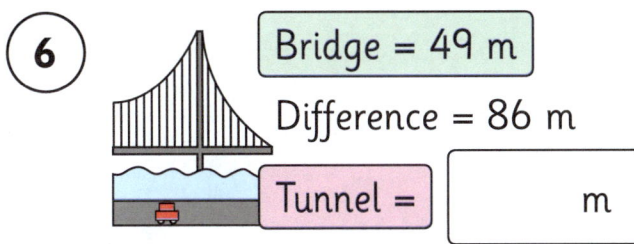
Bridge = 49 m
Difference = 86 m
Tunnel = ___ m

7.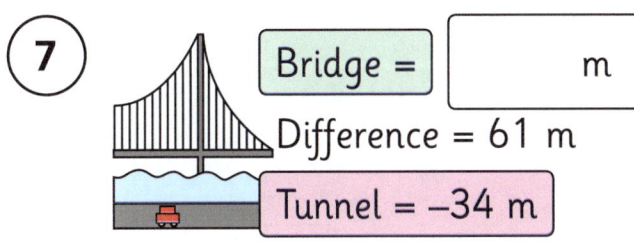
Bridge = ___ m
Difference = 61 m
Tunnel = −34 m

8.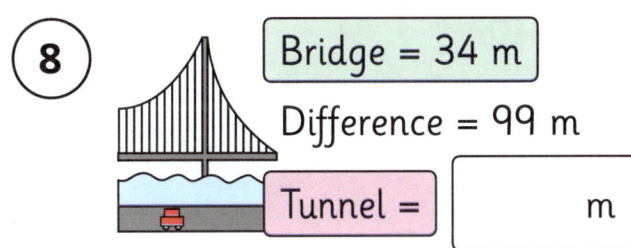
Bridge = 34 m
Difference = 99 m
Tunnel = ___ m

9.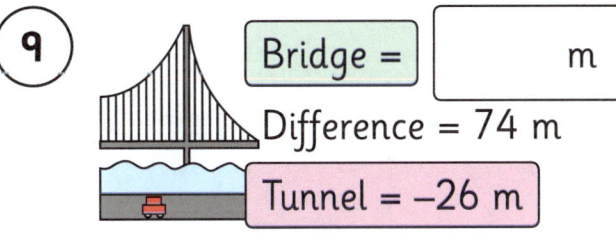
Bridge = ___ m
Difference = 74 m
Tunnel = −26 m

10.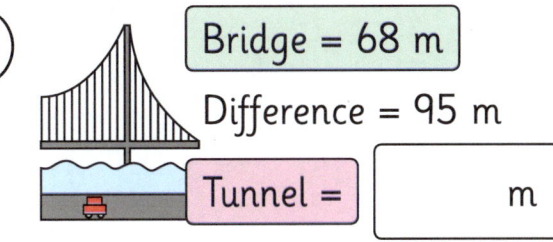
Bridge = 68 m
Difference = 95 m
Tunnel = ___ m

Today I scored ___ out of 10.

Week 1 — Day 4

Write the answer in its simplest form.

$\frac{1}{5} \div 2 = \boxed{\frac{1}{10}}$

1) $\frac{1}{4} \div 3 =$ ☐

2) $\frac{2}{5} \div 3 =$ ☐

3) $\frac{1}{6} \div 4 =$ ☐

4) $\frac{2}{3} \div 6 =$ ☐

5) $\frac{7}{9} \div 5 =$ ☐

6) $\frac{5}{7} \div 4 =$ ☐

7) $\frac{3}{4} \div 8 =$ ☐

8) $\frac{5}{8} \div 6 =$ ☐

9) $\frac{3}{7} \div 8 =$ ☐

10) $\frac{4}{6} \div 7 =$ ☐

11) $\frac{6}{8} \div 9 =$ ☐

12) $\frac{6}{7} \div 9 =$ ☐

Today I scored ☐ out of 12.

Week 1 — Day 5

Multiply the fractions to work out the answer. Give the answer in its simplest form.

At a kennel, $\frac{2}{3}$ of dogs are small. $\frac{3}{4}$ of the small dogs are brown. What fraction of dogs are small and brown?

$\frac{1}{2}$

1. In a wood, $\frac{7}{8}$ of animals are brown. $\frac{1}{4}$ of the brown animals have wings. What fraction of animals are brown and have wings?

2. At a zoo, $\frac{1}{5}$ of animals are stripy. $\frac{3}{8}$ of the stripy animals eat meat. What fraction of animals are stripy and eat meat?

3. In a pond, $\frac{5}{8}$ of fish are orange. $\frac{6}{10}$ of the orange fish are spotty. What fraction of fish are orange and spotty?

4. On safari, $\frac{8}{12}$ of animals are big. $\frac{3}{4}$ of the big animals have big teeth. What fraction of animals are big and have big teeth?

5. In a field, $\frac{3}{6}$ of animals are sheep. $\frac{1}{4}$ of the sheep are white. What fraction of animals are white sheep?

6. On a beach, $\frac{8}{10}$ of animals are crabs. $\frac{2}{3}$ of the crabs live in shells. What fraction of animals are crabs and live in shells?

7. In space, $\frac{2}{6}$ of aliens are green. $\frac{5}{6}$ of the green aliens have one eye. What fraction of aliens are green and have one eye?

8. In a pet shop, $\frac{4}{10}$ of pets are birds. $\frac{9}{12}$ of the birds can talk. What fraction of pets are birds and can talk?

Today I scored ☐ out of 8.

Week 2 — Day 1

Write the answer to the calculation.   4.13 × 2 = 8.26

1) 2.24 × 2 =
2) 3.1 × 5 =
3) 3.23 × 3 =
4) 8.02 × 2 =
5) 7.33 × 3 =
6) 5.12 × 4 =
7) 6.26 × 2 =
8) 2.09 × 9 =
9) 8.41 × 5 =
10) 4.39 × 4 =
11) 5.72 × 6 =
12) 7.18 × 8 =

Today I scored ☐ out of 12.

Week 2 — Day 2

Fill in the missing measurement.

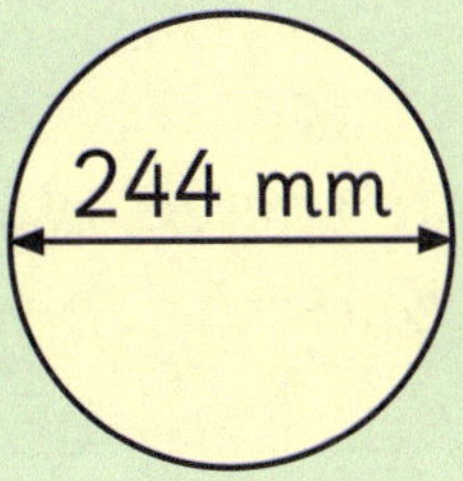

244 mm circle, radius = **12.2** cm

1. 1.2 m diameter — radius = ____ cm 
2. 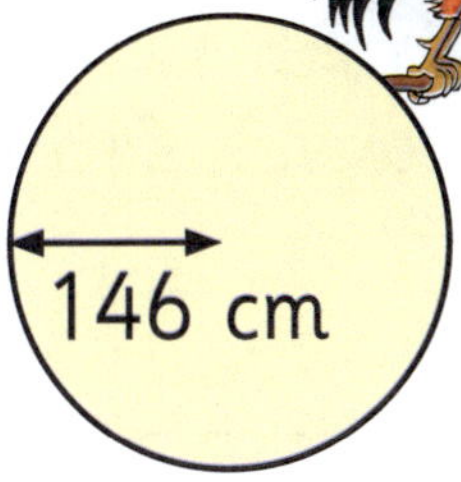 146 cm diameter — diameter = ____ m
3. 190 cm radius — diameter = ____ mm
4. 452 m diameter — radius = ____ cm
5. 358 mm radius — diameter = ____ cm
6. 1036 cm diameter — radius = ____ mm 
7. 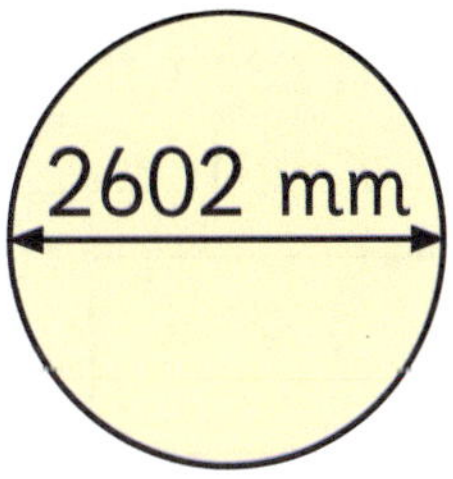 2602 mm diameter — radius = ____ cm
8. 1933 cm radius — diameter = ____ m

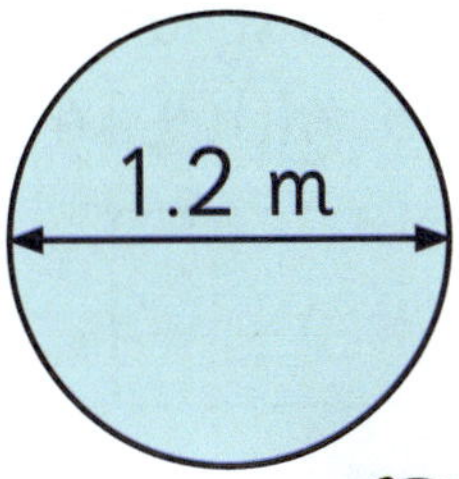

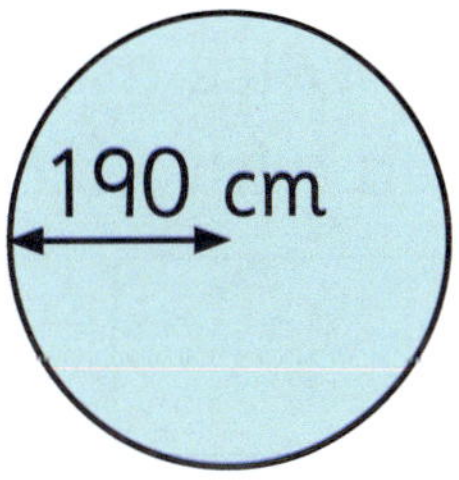

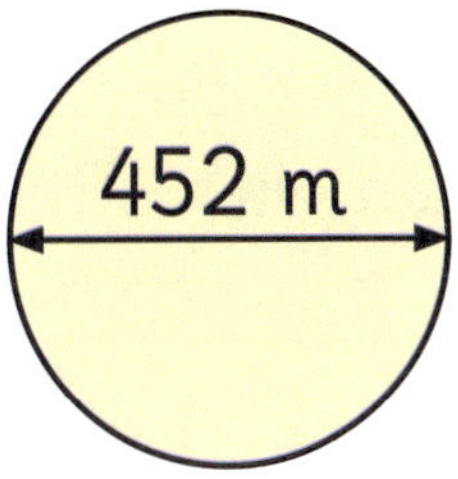

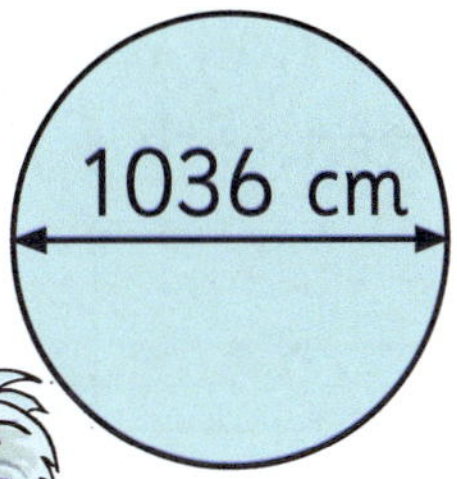

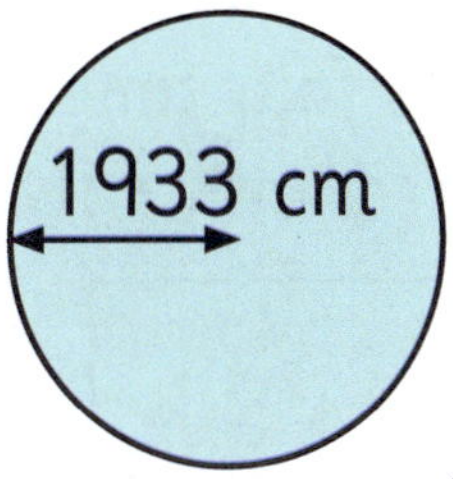

Today I scored ____ out of 8.

Week 2 — Day 3

How much money will Amie have left?

Hassan spends £1.40. Amie spends twice as much. She started with £10.

 £7.20

(1) Hassan spends £2.30. Amie spends twice as much. She started with £11.

£

(5) Hassan spends £6.36. Amie spends half as much. She started with £14.40.

£

(2) Hassan spends £4.80. Amie spends half as much. She started with £13.

£

(6) Hassan spends £9.39. Amie spends a third of that. She started with £15.45.

£

(3) Hassan spends £1.21. Amie spends three times more. She started with £12.90.

£

(7) Hassan spends £1.97. Amie spends twice as much. She started with £8.60.

£

(4) Hassan spends £2.26. Amie spends four times more. She started with £10.30.

£

(8) Hassan spends £0.96. Amie spends five times more. She started with £9.50.

£

Today I scored [ ] out of 8.

Week 2 — Day 4

Write the equivalent fraction to the fraction given, and then convert the fraction to a decimal.

$\frac{8}{20} = \frac{\boxed{4}}{10} = \boxed{0.4}$

1) $\frac{3}{5} = \frac{\Box}{10} = \Box$

2) $\frac{6}{20} = \frac{\Box}{10} = \Box$

3) $\frac{12}{20} = \frac{\Box}{100} = \Box$

4) $\frac{35}{50} = \frac{\Box}{100} = \Box$

5) $\frac{27}{30} = \frac{\Box}{10} = \Box$

6) $\frac{16}{40} = \frac{\Box}{10} = \Box$

7) $\frac{21}{30} = \frac{\Box}{10} = \Box$

8) $\frac{3}{25} = \frac{\Box}{100} = \Box$

9) $\frac{48}{60} = \frac{\Box}{10} = \Box$

10) $\frac{21}{25} = \frac{\Box}{100} = \Box$

11) $\frac{6}{200} = \frac{\Box}{100} = \Box$

12) $\frac{44}{400} = \frac{\Box}{100} = \Box$

Today I scored ☐ out of 12.

Week 2 — Day 5

Milo takes a journey which involves 3 trains. How long is Milo on the third train for?

All Trains: 2 hours 47 minutes
Train 1: 23 minutes
Train 2: 44 minutes
Train 3: **1** h **40** minutes

1) All Trains: 1 hour 59 minutes
Train 1: 74 minutes
Train 2: 23 minutes
Train 3: ___ minutes

2) All Trains: 2 hours 13 minutes
Train 1: 54 minutes
Train 2: 17 minutes
Train 3: ___ minutes

3) All Trains: 2 hours 38 minutes
Train 1: 45 minutes
Train 2: 46 minutes
Train 3: ___ minutes

4) All Trains: 4 hours 19 minutes
Train 1: 58 minutes
Train 2: 96 minutes
Train 3: ___ minutes

5) All Trains: 2 hours 52 minutes
Train 1: 41 minutes
Train 2: 53 minutes
Train 3: ___ h ___ minutes

6) All Trains: 2 hours 30 minutes
Train 1: 15 minutes
Train 2: 39 minutes
Train 3: ___ h ___ minutes

7) All Trains: 3 hours 25 minutes
Train 1: 64 minutes
Train 2: 37 minutes
Train 3: ___ h ___ minutes

8) All Trains: 5 hours 2 minutes
Train 1: 85 minutes
Train 2: 71 minutes
Train 3: ___ h ___ minutes

Today I scored ___ out of 8.

Week 3 — Day 1

Complete the calculation.   8.02 × |1000| = 8020

1) 3.63 × ☐ = 36.3

2) 419 ÷ ☐ = 41.9

3) 0.286 × ☐ = 2.86

4) 35.2 × ☐ = 3520

5) 5.21 × ☐ = 5210

6) 12.4 × ☐ = 12 400

7) 2.34 ÷ ☐ = 0.234

8) 829 ÷ ☐ = 8.29

9) 7270 ÷ ☐ = 7.27

10) 0.349 × ☐ = 34.9

11) 0.972 × ☐ = 972

12) 653 ÷ ☐ = 0.653

Today I scored ☐ out of 12.

Week 3 — Day 2

Fill in the boxes to show how many squares shape A has been translated to get shape B.

[5] right
[2] up

1) [ ] right [ ] down

2) [ ] left [ ] down

3) [ ] left [ ] up

4) [ ] right [ ] down

5) [ ] right [ ] down

6) [ ] left [ ] down

7) [ ] right [ ] up

8) [ ] right [ ] down

Today I scored [ ] out of 8.

Week 3 — Day 3

Write the name of the person who spends more money.

Jemma has £100. She spends 50% of it at the supermarket. Luna spends £40 at the supermarket.

Jemma

1. Josh has £200. He spends 50% of it on a new phone. Lisa spends £90 on a new phone.

2. Kamala has £100. She spends 35% of it at a restaurant. Nakia spends £30 at a restaurant.

3. Paula has £500. She spends 10% of it on a video game. Samuel spends £60 on a video game.

4. Christine has £400. She spends 25% of it on a bike. Louisa spends £120 on a bike.

5. Katie has £700. She spends 2% of it on a book. Marvin spends £15 on a book.

6. Stefan has £600. He spends 60% of it on a TV. Rafael spends £320 on a TV.

7. Chloe has £900. She spends 60% of it on a plane ticket. Kian spends £600 on a plane ticket.

8. Dylan has £900. He spends 5% of it on new clothes. Raj spends £56 on new clothes.

Today I scored ☐ out of 8.

Week 3 — Day 4

Complete the number sentence by writing =, < or > in each box.

$\frac{47}{100}$ > 0.45 < 46%

1) 74% ☐ $\frac{72}{100}$ ☐ 0.76

2) 0.55 ☐ 45% ☐ $\frac{1}{2}$

3) 32% ☐ $\frac{33}{100}$ ☐ 0.31

4) $\frac{3}{4}$ ☐ 76% ☐ 0.77

5) $\frac{9}{10}$ ☐ 0.11 ☐ 10%

6) 0.81 ☐ $\frac{8}{100}$ ☐ 79%

7) $\frac{4}{100}$ ☐ 3% ☐ 0.2

8) 0.04 ☐ $\frac{5}{100}$ ☐ 30%

9) 0.09 ☐ 9% ☐ $\frac{7}{10}$

10) 0.16 ☐ $\frac{3}{50}$ ☐ 60%

11) $\frac{1}{5}$ ☐ 20% ☐ 0.18

12) 0.06 ☐ $\frac{3}{5}$ ☐ 53%

Today I scored ☐ out of 12.

Week 3 — Day 5

A bag contains only blue, orange and pink sweets. What percentage of the sweets are pink?

Blue	Orange	Pink
30%	$\frac{9}{100}$	61%

1.

Blue	Orange	Pink
50%	$\frac{30}{100}$	%

2.

Blue	Orange	Pink
28%	$\frac{22}{100}$	%

3.

Blue	Orange	Pink
12%	$\frac{17}{100}$	%

4.

Blue	Orange	Pink
10%	$\frac{6}{10}$	%

5.

Blue	Orange	Pink
52%	$\frac{1}{4}$	%

6.

Blue	Orange	Pink
63%	$\frac{2}{10}$	%

7.

Blue	Orange	Pink
14%	$\frac{3}{4}$	%

8.

Blue	Orange	Pink
8%	$\frac{27}{50}$	%

9.

Blue	Orange	Pink
28%	$\frac{8}{25}$	%

10.

Blue	Orange	Pink
19%	$\frac{7}{20}$	%

Today I scored ☐ out of 10.

Week 4 — Day 1

Complete the sentence about the named shape.

Regular heptagon: I have **7** obtuse angle(s) and **0** right angle(s).

1. Square — I have ☐ obtuse angle(s) and ☐ right angle(s).

2. Regular hexagon — I have ☐ obtuse angle(s) and ☐ right angle(s).

3. Regular octagon — I have ☐ obtuse angle(s) and ☐ right angle(s).

4. Equilateral triangle — I have ☐ obtuse angle(s) and ☐ right angle(s).

5. Rectangle — I have ☐ obtuse angle(s) and ☐ right angle(s).

6. Right-angled triangle — I have ☐ obtuse angle(s) and ☐ right angle(s).

7. Parallelogram — I have ☐ obtuse angle(s) and ☐ right angle(s).

8. Rhombus — I have ☐ obtuse angle(s) and ☐ right angle(s).

Today I scored ☐ out of 8.

Week 4 — Day 2

Circle the three common multiples of the numbers in the pink box.

8 and 5

(40) 60 (160)
45   35 (80)

1	3 and 4	12	28	16	24	36	9
2	7 and 10	720	280	70	30	540	490
3	6 and 4	36	42	240	20	18	48
4	4 and 5	60	15	20	45	30	80
5	9 and 2	54	28	36	45	90	64
6	7 and 2	21	560	42	320	24	84
7	12 and 8	240	60	84	480	32	96
8	11 and 3	33	44	36	66	99	77
9	9 and 12	360	54	108	48	120	72

Today I scored ☐ out of 9.

Week 4 — Day 3

Solve the calculation. $\frac{2}{5} \times 400 = $ 160

1) $\frac{1}{2} \times 180 = $

2) $\frac{1}{4} \times 280 = $

3) $\frac{7}{8} \times 800 = $

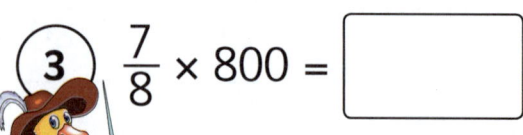

4) $\frac{2}{3} \times 240 = $

5) $\frac{9}{10} \times 600 = $

6) $\frac{3}{4} \times 360 = $

7) $\frac{5}{6} \times 300 = $

8) $\frac{3}{5} \times 550 = $

9) $\frac{6}{11} \times 220 = $

10) $\frac{2}{7} \times 490 = $

11) $\frac{4}{9} \times 720 = $

12) $\frac{7}{12} \times 840 = $

Today I scored ☐ out of 12.

Week 4 — Day 4

How many stickers does each person get?

Amir and Lucy share 24 stickers in the ratio 1 : 2.
Amir: 8   Lucy: 16

1 Sady and Job share 25 stickers in the ratio 4 : 1.
Sady: Job:

2 Ezra and Jung share 48 stickers in the ratio 1 : 3.
Ezra: Jung:

3 Tara and Sean share 36 stickers in the ratio 2 : 4.
Tara: Sean:

4 Mika and Han share 70 stickers in the ratio 4 : 3.
Mika: Han:

5 Leah and Pria share 60 stickers in the ratio 5 : 7.
Leah: Pria:

6 Cole and Demi share 64 stickers in the ratio 3 : 5.
Cole: Demi:

7 Rae and Theo share 88 stickers in the ratio 4 : 7.
Rae: Theo:

8 Sahar and Neil share 81 stickers in the ratio 6 : 3.
Sahar: Neil:

Today I scored ___ out of 8.

Week 4 — Day 5

Complete the sentence. For every 4 potatoes a farmer grows, she grows 1 carrot. If the farmer grows 400 potatoes, she grows [100] carrots.

1. For every 1 pumpkin a farmer grows, she grows 2 turnips.
   If the farmer grows 120 pumpkins, she grows [ ] turnips.

2. For every 3 peppers a farmer grows, she grows 1 courgette.
   If the farmer grows 330 peppers, she grows [ ] courgettes.

3. For every 2 parsnips a farmer grows, she grows 3 onions.
   If the farmer grows 140 parsnips, she grows [ ] onions.

4. For every 9 peas a farmer grows, she grows 2 leeks.
   If the farmer grows 540 peas, she grows [ ] leeks.

5. For every 7 cabbages a farmer grows, she grows 2 tomatoes.
   If the farmer grows 630 cabbages, she grows [ ] tomatoes.

6. For every 6 cucumbers a farmer grows, she grows 11 cauliflowers.
   If the farmer grows 420 cucumbers, she grows [ ] cauliflowers.

7. For every 4 radishes a farmer grows, she grows 7 sprouts.
   If the farmer grows 480 radishes, she grows [ ] sprouts.

8. For every 12 beans a farmer grows, she grows 8 aubergines.
   If the farmer grows 720 beans, she grows [ ] aubergines.

Today I scored [ ] out of 8.

Week 5 — Day 1

Complete the sentence. 8 648 153 rounded to the nearest 100 000 is **8 600 000**.

1) 9 823 509 rounded to the nearest 1000 is ☐.

2) 7 901 524 rounded to the nearest 1000 is ☐.

3) 440 700 rounded to the nearest 100 000 is ☐.

4) 147 300 rounded to the nearest 10 000 is ☐.

5) 5 768 140 rounded to the nearest 10 000 is ☐.

6) 2 235 790 rounded to the nearest 100 000 is ☐.

7) 6 345 242 rounded to the nearest 100 000 is ☐.

8) 1 234 689 rounded to the nearest 10 000 is ☐.

9) 3 454 562 rounded to the nearest 10 000 is ☐.

Today I scored ☐ out of 9.

Week 5 — Day 2

Complete the sentence. If an apple costs 60p, 4 apples will cost £2.40.

1. If an apple costs 90p, 10 apples will cost £ ☐.

2. If an apple costs 30p, 7 apples will cost £ ☐.

3. If an apple costs 50p, 6 apples will cost £ ☐.

4. If an apple costs 40p, 11 apples will cost £ ☐.

5. If an apple costs 60p, 8 apples will cost £ ☐.

6. If an apple costs 70p, 9 apples will cost £ ☐.

7. If an apple costs 80p, 8 apples will cost £ ☐.

8. If an apple costs 15p, 5 apples will cost £ ☐.

9. If an apple costs 20p, 18 apples will cost £ ☐.

10. If an apple costs 25p, 8 apples will cost £ ☐.

11. If an apple costs 12p, 12 apples will cost £ ☐.

12. If an apple costs 90p, 12 apples will cost £ ☐.

Today I scored ☐ out of 12.

Week 5 — Day 3

What is the scale factor of enlargement from the smaller shape to the bigger shape?

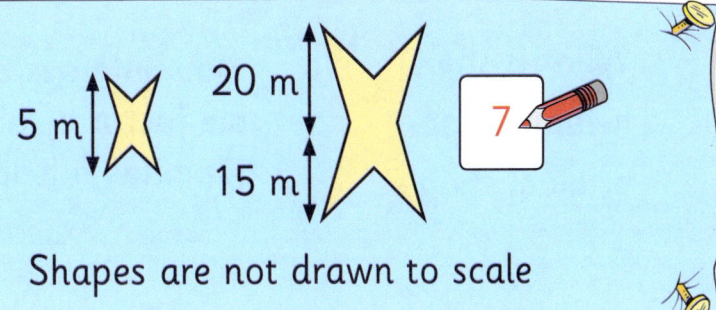

Shapes are not drawn to scale

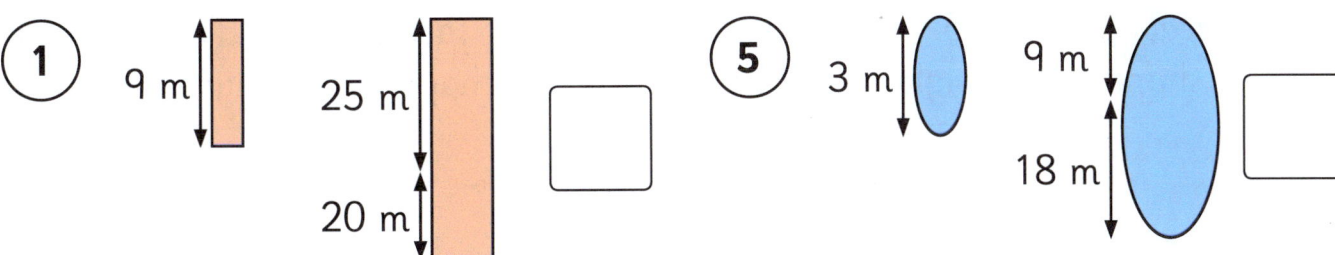

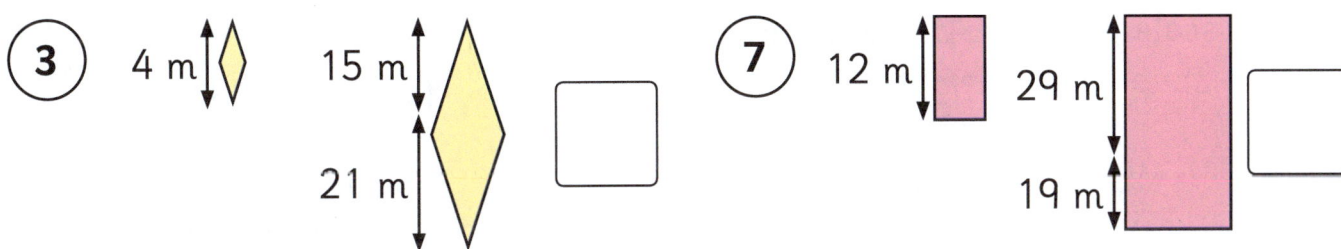

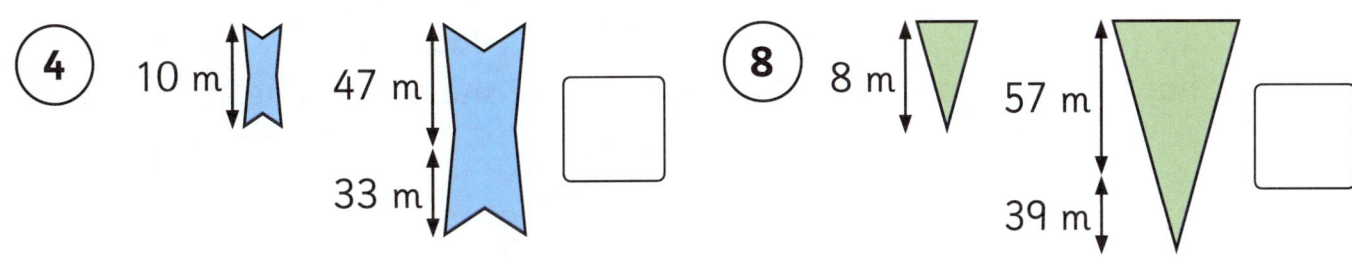

Today I scored ☐ out of 8.

Week 5 — Day 4

What is the height of the original shape?

Bob enlarges a shape by a scale factor of 6. The enlarged shape has a height of 0.54 m.

9 cm

1) Leo enlarges a shape by a scale factor of 5. The enlarged shape has a height of 0.25 m.

☐ cm

2) Alia enlarges a shape by a scale factor of 9. The enlarged shape has a height of 0.9 m.

☐ cm

3) Chase enlarges a shape by a scale factor of 4. The enlarged shape has a height of 0.32 m.

☐ cm

4) Mary enlarges a shape by a scale factor of 12. The enlarged shape has a height of 0.84 m.

☐ cm

5) Jon enlarges a shape by a scale factor of 11. The enlarged shape has a height of 1.21 m.

☐ cm

6) Aled enlarges a shape by a scale factor of 9. The enlarged shape has a height of 1.08 m.

☐ cm

7) Ash enlarges a shape by a scale factor of 14. The enlarged shape has a height of 2.8 m.

☐ cm

8) Tino enlarges a shape by a scale factor of 25. The enlarged shape has a height of 1.5 m.

☐ cm

Today I scored ☐ out of 8.

Week 5 — Day 5

3 out of every 5 ice cream cones Iris sells are strawberry. Find the missing value.

Total cones sold: 20
Strawberry cones sold: **?**

? = 12

1) Total cones sold: 50
   Strawberry cones sold: **?**
   ? =

2) Total cones sold: **?**
   Strawberry cones sold: 6
   ? =

3) Total cones sold: 45
   Strawberry cones sold: **?**
   ? =

4) Total cones sold: 100
   Strawberry cones sold: **?**
   ? =

5) Total cones sold: **?**
   Strawberry cones sold: 15
   ? =

6) Total cones sold: **?**
   Strawberry cones sold: 90
   ? =

7) Total cones sold: 60
   Strawberry cones sold: **?**
   ? =

8) Total cones sold: **?**
   Strawberry cones sold: 33
   ? =

9) Total cones sold: 65
   Strawberry cones sold: **?**
   ? =

10) Total cones sold: 70
    Strawberry cones sold: **?**
    ? =

11) Total cones sold: 80
    Strawberry cones sold: **?**
    ? =

12) Total cones sold: 110
    Strawberry cones sold: **?**
    ? =

Today I scored ☐ out of 12.

Week 6 — Day 1

Circle the number that correctly completes the sentence.

4 623 712 is larger than **?**

| 4 632 918 | (4 362 156) |

1) 2 759 283 is smaller than **?**
   | 3 645 109 | 1 981 418 |

2) 3 127 809 is larger than **?**
   | 3 098 678 | 3 132 092 |

3) 2 531 259 is smaller than **?**
   | 2 543 156 | 2 512 008 |

4) 891 675 is larger than **?**
   | 891 841 | 891 498 |

5) 1 235 632 is smaller than **?**
   | 1 235 718 | 1 235 435 |

6) 7 043 151 is smaller than **?**
   | 7 304 142 | 7 034 169 |

7) 9 546 279 is larger than **?**
   | 9 546 292 | 9 546 265 |

8) 5 091 517 is smaller than **?**
   | 5 910 283 | 5 019 810 |

9) 9 609 122 is smaller than **?**
   | 9 690 122 | 9 096 022 |

10) 4 508 070 is larger than **?**
    | 4 508 700 | 4 508 007 |

11) 6 544 181 is larger than **?**
    | 6 544 118 | 6 544 811 |

12) 2 253 198 is larger than **?**
    | 2 235 198 | 2 325 198 |

Today I scored ☐ out of 12.

Week 6 — Day 2

Complete the sequence. 17, 21, 25, 29, 33

1. 35, 31, 27, ___, ___
2. −10, −5, 0, ___, ___
3. −8, −11, −14, ___, ___
4. ___, ___, 13, 16, 19
5. ___, ___, 14, 9, 4
6. ___, ___, 19, 25, 31
7. −12, ___, ___, 0, 4
8. 5, ___, ___, −1, −3
9. ___, 18, 25, ___, 39
10. −7, ___, ___, 2, 5
11. 23, ___, ___, 56, 67
12. ___, 38, 26, ___, 2

Today I scored ___ out of 12.

Week 6 — Day 3

Fill in the fourth term of the sequence and write the rule for the sequence in the box.

$1\frac{3}{4}$ | 2 | $2\frac{1}{4}$ | $2\frac{2}{4}$ Rule: add $\frac{1}{4}$

1 $1\frac{1}{2}$ | 2 | $2\frac{1}{2}$ | ☐
Rule:

5 $2\frac{5}{8}$ | $2\frac{3}{8}$ | $2\frac{1}{8}$ | ☐
Rule:

2 $5\frac{1}{4}$ | 5 | $4\frac{3}{4}$ | ☐
Rule:

6 $4\frac{4}{7}$ | $3\frac{6}{7}$ | $3\frac{1}{7}$ | ☐
Rule:

3 $2\frac{1}{3}$ | 3 | $3\frac{2}{3}$ | ☐
Rule:

7 $3\frac{7}{9}$ | $4\frac{2}{9}$ | $4\frac{6}{9}$ | ☐
Rule:

4 $3\frac{4}{5}$ | $4\frac{1}{5}$ | $4\frac{3}{5}$ | ☐
Rule:

8 $7\frac{1}{6}$ | $6\frac{2}{6}$ | $5\frac{3}{6}$ | ☐
Rule:

Today I scored ☐ out of 8.

Week 6 — Day 4

The formula for the term in position n of a sequence is given. Work out the value of the given term in the sequence.

$3n - 1$ The 5th term in the sequence → 14

1. $2n - 3$ The 2nd term in the sequence →

2. $5n + 2$ The 3rd term in the sequence →

3. $4n + 7$ The 1st term in the sequence →

4. $6n + 8$ The 5th term in the sequence →

5. $2n + 12$ The 4th term in the sequence →

6. $4n + 5$ The 4th term in the sequence →

7. $3n - 12$ The 3rd term in the sequence →

8. $7n - 11$ The 8th term in the sequence →

9. $8n - 9$ The 6th term in the sequence →

10. $9n + 10$ The 12th term in the sequence →

Today I scored ☐ out of 10.

Week 6 — Day 5

Use the formula to complete the sentence.

Amount of flour = 8 g × Number of cookies + 20 g

The amount of flour needed to make 5 cookies is 60 g.

1 Amount of flour = 120 g × Number of chocolate cakes + 50 g

The amount of flour needed to make 2 chocolate cakes is ☐ g.

2 Amount of flour = 10 g × Number of pancakes + 15 g

The amount of flour needed to make 16 pancakes is ☐ g.

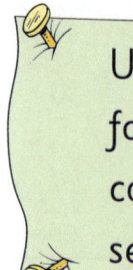

3 Amount of flour = 200 g × Number of carrot cakes − 70 g

The amount of flour needed to make 4 carrot cakes is ☐ g.

4 Amount of flour = 150 g × Number of sponge cakes + 110 g

The amount of flour needed to make 3 sponge cakes is ☐ g.

5 Amount of flour = 9 g × Number of brownies + 25 g

The amount of flour needed to make 7 brownies is ☐ g.

6 Amount of flour = 90 g × Number of vanilla cakes + 80 g

The amount of flour needed to make 6 vanilla cakes is ☐ g.

7 Amount of flour = 11 g × Number of cupcakes − 10 g

The amount of flour needed to make 12 cupcakes is ☐ g.

Today I scored ☐ out of 7.

Week 7 — Day 1

Use the equation to work out the value of the shape.

★ ÷ 9 + 9 = 11

★ = 18

1) 2 × △ = 20
   △ =

2) 3 × ◯ = 36
   ◯ =

3) 6 × ■ − 12 = 18
   ■ =

4) ⬠ ÷ 3 + 10 = 19
   ⬠ =

5) ★ ÷ 4 + 9 = 21
   ★ =

6) 5 × ▽ − 18 = 32
   ▽ =

7) 4 × ■ − 7 = 29
   ■ =

8) ⬠ ÷ 6 + 15 = 22
   ⬠ =

9) 8 × △ − 15 = 81
   △ =

10) 9 × ◯ + 8 = 71
    ◯ =

11) ▽ ÷ 9 − 5 = 4
    ▽ =

12) ★ ÷ 11 + 11 = 23
    ★ =

Today I scored ☐ out of 12.

Week 7 — Day 2

Solve the calculation. $1\frac{1}{2} + 2\frac{1}{4} = \boxed{3\frac{3}{4}}$

1) $2\frac{1}{2} + 2\frac{1}{6} =$

2) $\frac{5}{6} + 2\frac{1}{12} =$

3) $1\frac{1}{3} + 5\frac{1}{6} =$

4) $1\frac{3}{4} + 3\frac{1}{8} =$

5) $1\frac{1}{3} + 2\frac{5}{9} =$

6) $6\frac{3}{10} + 2\frac{9}{20} =$

7) $7\frac{1}{2} + 5\frac{3}{8} =$

8) $2\frac{1}{3} + 3\frac{5}{12} =$

9) $8\frac{1}{4} + 2\frac{7}{12} =$

10) $6\frac{2}{5} + 3\frac{11}{20} =$

11) $2\frac{5}{7} + 2\frac{5}{14} =$

12) $2\frac{7}{9} + 1\frac{5}{18} =$

Today I scored ☐ out of 12.

Week 7 — Day 3

Circle the equation for which both pairs of values are true.

$x = 3$ and $y = 2$
$x = 4$ and $y = 1$

| $2x + y = 10$ | $x - y = 1$ | (x + y = 5) |

1) $x = 1$ and $y = 4$; $x = 2$ and $y = 2$
| $2x + y = 6$ | $3x + 2y = 11$ | $x + 3y = 8$ |

2) $x = 2$ and $y = 4$; $x = 3$ and $y = 3$
| $3x + y = 12$ | $2x - y = 0$ | $x + y = 6$ |

3) $x = 2$ and $y = 3$; $x = 3$ and $y = 5$
| $x + 2y = 8$ | $2x - y = 1$ | $x + y = 8$ |

4) $x = 5$ and $y = 2$; $x = 7$ and $y = 4$
| $x - y = 3$ | $2x + y = 12$ | $x + 3y = 19$ |

5) $x = 6$ and $y = 8$; $x = 4$ and $y = 2$
| $2x + y = 20$ | $3x - y = 10$ | $x + y = 6$ |

6) $x = 8$ and $y = 2$; $x = 6$ and $y = 4$
| $x - y = 2$ | $x + 2y = 12$ | $2x + 2y = 20$ |

7) $x = 6$ and $y = 6$; $x = 7$ and $y = 9$
| $2x + y = 18$ | $3x - y = 12$ | $2x + 2y = 32$ |

8) $x = 2$ and $y = 5$; $x = 4$ and $y = 2$
| $3x + 2y = 16$ | $2x + 2y = 14$ | $2x - 3y = 2$ |

Today I scored ☐ out of 8.

Week 7 — Day 4

The letters in the equation stand for whole numbers greater than 0. List the 3 possible pairs of values of A and B.

$4A + B = 16$

A = 1   B = 12
A = 2   B = 8
A = 3   B = 4

1) $A + B = 4$

A =   B =
A =   B =
A =   B =

4) $2A + B = 8$

A =   B =
A =   B =
A =   B =

2) $A \times B = 9$

A =   B =
A =   B =
A =   B =

5) $A + 3B = 10$

A =   B =
A =   B =
A =   B =

3) $2A \times B = 8$

A =   B =
A =   B =
A =   B =

6) $3A + 2B = 24$

A =   B =
A =   B =
A =   B =

Today I scored ☐ out of 6.

Week 7 — Day 5

Using the information given, write an equation linking x and y. Then complete the sentence with the value of y.

If you multiply x by 5 and add 4 you get y. $y = 5x + 4$

When x = 4, y = 24.

1) If you multiply x by 10 you get y.   When x = 3, y = ___.

2) If you multiply x by 6 you get y.   When x = 6, y = ___.

3) If you multiply x by 3 and add 2 you get y.   When x = 2, y = ___.

4) If you multiply x by 2 and subtract 4 you get y.   When x = 4, y = ___.

5) If you multiply x by 4 and add 12 you get y.   When x = 8, y = ___.

6) If you multiply x by 7 and add 5 you get y.   When x = 5, y = ___.

7) If you multiply x by 9 and add 11 you get y.   When x = 7, y = ___.

8) If you multiply x by 8 and subtract 6 you get y.   When x = 9, y = ___.

9) If you multiply x by 12 and subtract 8 you get y.   When x = 7, y = ___.

Today I scored ___ out of 9.

Week 8 — Day 1

How much does the shopper spend?   Roshan buys 6 toy cars costing £4.03 each.   £24.18

1. Rowan buys 10 lollipops costing £0.25 each.
£

2. Elsie buys 2 plants costing £8.25 each.
£

3. Zafira buys 9 balls costing £2.05 each.
£

4. Nevin buys 4 pens costing £1.12 each.
£

5. Hugh buys 11 kites costing £5.09 each.
£

6. Nico buys 12 cards costing £1.07 each.
£

7. Luke buys 8 comics costing £2.12 each.
£

8. Joe buys 3 posters costing £6.15 each.
£

9. Renée buys 3 stamps costing £1.29 each.
£

10. Adele buys 6 T-shirts costing £4.20 each.
£

11. Tomas buys 5 dolls costing £3.50 each.
£

12. Hafsah buys 7 books costing £7.99 each.
£

Today I scored ☐ out of 12.

Week 8 — Day 2

Convert the distance into the units given.   1905 m = **1.905** km

1) 4.125 km = _____ m

2) 195.6 cm = _____ m

3) 1.722 km = _____ m

4) 2.431 m = _____ cm

5) 7563 m = _____ km

6) 25.03 cm = _____ mm

7) 3486 m = _____ km

8) 6.391 cm = _____ mm

9) 3914 mm = _____ cm

10) 8235 cm = _____ m

11) 723.4 mm = _____ cm

12) 50.91 m = _____ cm

Today I scored _____ out of 12.

Week 8 — Day 3

Fill in the box with <, > or =.   309.5 cm > 3078 mm

1. 1.658 km ☐ 1658 m
2. 231.2 cm ☐ 2.213 m
3. 7621 m ☐ 7.612 km
4. 48.19 mm ☐ 4.819 cm
5. 2.053 cm ☐ 20.35 mm
6. 912.6 cm ☐ 9216 mm

7. 3785 cm ☐ 37.58 m
8. 5.687 m ☐ 567.8 cm
9. 0.812 km ☐ 8120 m
10. 7.949 cm ☐ 799.4 mm
11. 6307 mm ☐ 67.03 cm
12. 79.23 m ☐ 793.2 cm

Today I scored ☐ out of 12.

Week 8 — Day 4

How many laps of the park's perimeter will the person have to run to reach their goal?

Evan's goal is to run 3 km. The park's perimeter is 600 m.

5 laps

1. Mia's goal is to run 5 km. The park's perimeter is 500 m.
   ☐ laps

2. Lydia's goal is to run 3.2 km. The park's perimeter is 800 m.
   ☐ laps

3. John's goal is to run 4.5 km. The park's perimeter is 900 m.
   ☐ laps

4. Yasmine's goal is to run 3.6 km. The park's perimeter is 400 m.
   ☐ laps

5. Caleb's goal is to run 7.2 km. The park's perimeter is 900 m.
   ☐ laps

6. Jay's goal is to run 4.9 km. The park's perimeter is 700 m.
   ☐ laps

7. Mira's goal is to run 2.8 km. The park's perimeter is 200 m.
   ☐ laps

8. Kate's goal is to run 1.75 km. The park's perimeter is 250 m.
   ☐ laps

9. Lara's goal is to run 10.8 km. The park's perimeter is 900 m.
   ☐ laps

10. Rick's goal is to run 13.2 km. The park's perimeter is 1200 m.
    ☐ laps

Today I scored ☐ out of 10.

Week 8 — Day 5

8 km is approximately equal to 5 miles. The distances from A to B and B to C are given. Work out an approximation for the total distance from A to C in miles.

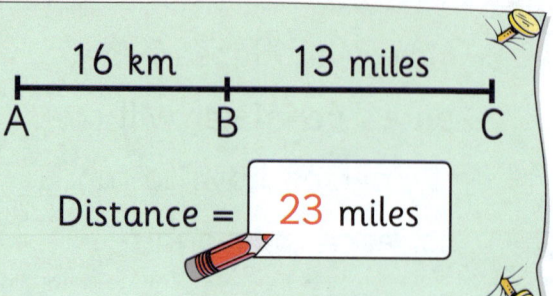

Distance = 23 miles

1)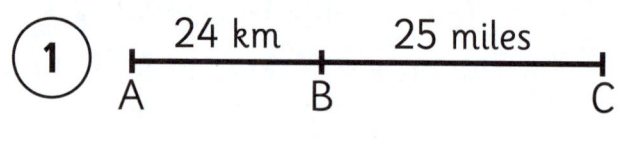

Distance = ____ miles

5)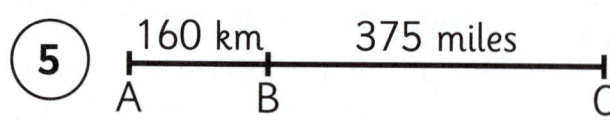

Distance = ____ miles

2)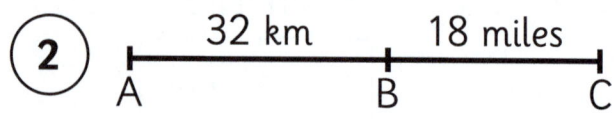

Distance = ____ miles

6)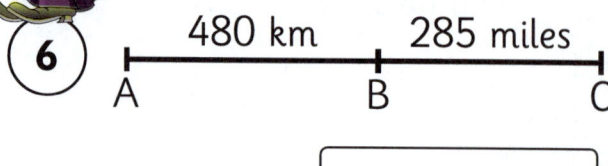

Distance = ____ miles

3)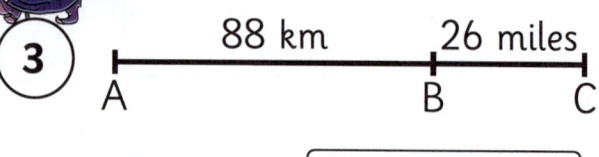

Distance = ____ miles

7)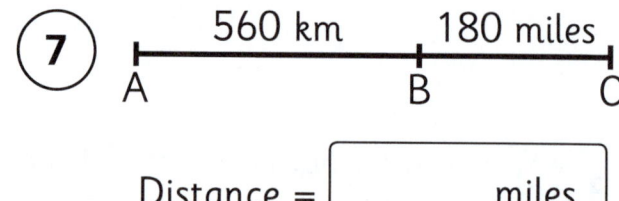

Distance = ____ miles

4)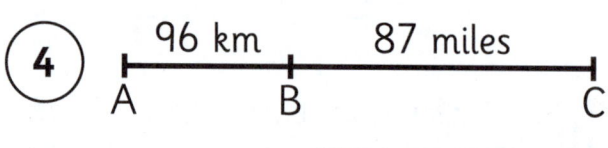

Distance = ____ miles

8)

Distance = ____ miles

Today I scored ____ out of 8.

Week 9 — Day 1

Solve the percentage calculation, giving your answer in grams.

70% of 8 kg = 5600 g

1) 50% of 5 kg = ☐ g
2) 10% of 6.5 kg = ☐ g
3) 60% of 4 kg = ☐ g
4) 20% of 9 kg = ☐ g
5) 2% of 4.1 kg = ☐ g
6) 25% of 0.8 kg = ☐ g
7) 30% of 3.2 kg = ☐ g
8) 12% of 7 kg = ☐ g
9) 9% of 1.2 kg = ☐ g
10) 15% of 3 kg = ☐ g
11) 3% of 8.2 kg = ☐ g
12) 78% of 2 kg = ☐ g

Today I scored ☐ out of 12.

Week 9 — Day 2

Convert the length of the journey into the units given.

Taylor was on the tram for 20 minutes. **1200** seconds

1) Asim's bus ride took 30 minutes.
   ☐ seconds

2) Cleo's drive to work took 50 minutes.
   ☐ seconds

3) Louis was on the ferry for 2 and a half hours.
   ☐ minutes

4) Ciara's flight took half a day.
   ☐ minutes

5) Sakina went on a cruise for 20 days.
   ☐ hours

6) Ria walked for 1 hour and 10 minutes.
   ☐ seconds

7) Rishi cycled for 2 hours.
   ☐ seconds

8) Matt drove for 3 hours and 20 minutes.
   ☐ seconds

9) Axel's train took 1 day and 16 hours.
   ☐ minutes

10) Olive sailed for 5 and a half days.
    ☐ hours

Today I scored ☐ out of 10.

Week 9 — Day 3

The table shows the volume of each drink Naomi drinks in a day. How many litres does she drink in total?

Drink	Volume
Water	1.75 l
Juice	250 ml
Tea	150 ml

2.15 l

1)
Drink	Volume
Water	3.21 l
Juice	1.12 l
Tea	350 ml

_____ l

2)
Drink	Volume
Water	2.15 l
Juice	1.05 l
Tea	320 ml

_____ l

3)
Drink	Volume
Water	2.35 l
Juice	120 ml
Tea	215 ml

_____ l

4)
Drink	Volume
Water	3.215 l
Juice	0.995 l
Tea	150 ml

_____ l

5)
Drink	Volume
Water	2.315 l
Juice	1.075 l
Tea	210 ml

_____ l

6)
Drink	Volume
Water	1.425 l
Juice	650 ml
Tea	135 ml

_____ l

7)
Drink	Volume
Water	3.025 l
Juice	332 ml
Tea	0.432 l

_____ l

8)
Drink	Volume
Water	3.124 l
Juice	763 ml
Tea	300 ml

_____ l

9)
Drink	Volume
Water	3.684 l
Juice	415 ml
Tea	200 ml

_____ l

10)
Drink	Volume
Water	2.999 l
Juice	782 ml
Tea	314 ml

_____ l

Today I scored ____ out of 10.

Week 9 — Day 4

How many weeks will it take the person to reach their savings goal?

Lea's savings goal is £140. She puts £4 into her piggy bank every day.

5 week(s)

1 Tim's savings goal is £280. He puts £1 into his piggy bank every day.

____ week(s)

2 Bea's savings goal is £210. She puts £30 into her piggy bank every day.

____ week(s)

3 Omar's savings goal is £630. He puts £10 into his piggy bank every day.

____ week(s)

4 Dean's savings goal is £560. He puts 80p into his piggy bank every day.

____ week(s)

5 Kara's savings goal is £700. She puts £5 into her piggy bank every day.

____ week(s)

6 Piper's savings goal is £840. She puts £20 into her piggy bank every day.

____ week(s)

7 Ron's savings goal is £70. He puts 20p into his piggy bank every day.

____ week(s)

8 Kadir's savings goal is £420. He puts £5 into his piggy bank every day.

____ week(s)

Today I scored ____ out of 8.

Week 9 — Day 5

Work out the value of the missing mass in grams.

420 g + 1.25 kg + ? = 2 kg

? = 330 g

1) 610 g + 2.13 kg + ? = 3 kg

? = ___ g

2) 150 g + 2.75 kg + ? = 4 kg

? = ___ g

3) 530 g + 4.35 kg + ? = 5 kg

? = ___ g

4) 260 g + 4.72 kg + ? = 7 kg

? = ___ g

5) 820 g + 1.21 kg + ? = 2.5 kg

? = ___ g

6) 995 g + 3.67 kg + ? = 6 kg

? = ___ g

7) 305 g + 6.92 kg + ? = 9 kg

? = ___ g

8) 730 g + 3.76 kg + ? = 7.5 kg

? = ___ g

Today I scored ___ out of 8.

Week 10 — Day 1

Complete the equivalent fraction of the fraction given.

$\frac{3}{4} = \frac{12}{16}$

1) $\frac{10}{3} = \frac{}{12}$

2) $\frac{4}{5} = \frac{}{35}$

3) $\frac{44}{16} = \frac{}{4}$

4) $\frac{9}{6} = \frac{}{42}$

5) $\frac{8}{9} = \frac{}{81}$

6) $\frac{6}{7} = \frac{}{84}$

7) $\frac{14}{4} = \frac{}{6}$

8) $\frac{8}{6} = \frac{}{9}$

9) $\frac{15}{6} = \frac{}{8}$

10) $\frac{12}{50} = \frac{}{75}$

11) $\frac{5}{25} = \frac{}{10}$

12) $\frac{32}{12} = \frac{}{9}$

Today I scored ☐ out of 12.

Week 10 — Day 2

Solve the calculation. Give your answer in its simplest form. $\frac{1}{2} \div 10 = \boxed{\frac{1}{20}}$

1) $\frac{1}{4} \div 2 =$

2) $\frac{3}{5} \div 10 =$

3) $\frac{5}{6} \div 5 =$

4) $\frac{2}{3} \div 3 =$

5) $\frac{4}{5} \div 4 =$

6) $\frac{7}{8} \div 8 =$

7) $\frac{4}{7} \div 6 =$

8) $\frac{5}{9} \div 9 =$

9) $\frac{4}{11} \div 8 =$

10) $\frac{2}{9} \div 7 =$

11) $\frac{3}{8} \div 12 =$

12) $\frac{4}{12} \div 9 =$

Today I scored ☐ out of 12.

Week 10 — Day 3

Work out the sizes of angles a, b and c.

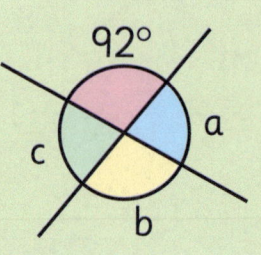

a = 88°
b = 92°
c = 88°

1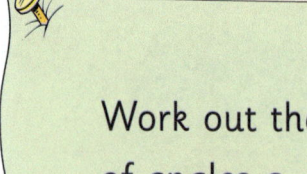

a = ___°
b = ___°
c = ___°

5

a = ___°
b = ___°
c = ___°

2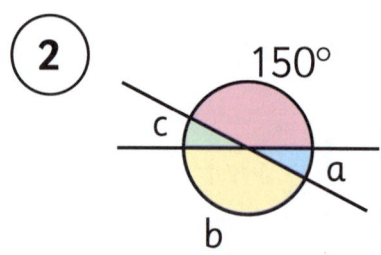

a = ___°
b = ___°
c = ___°

6

a = ___°
b = ___°
c = ___°

3

a = ___°
b = ___°
c = ___°

7

a = ___°
b = ___°
c = ___°

4

a = ___°
b = ___°
c = ___°

8

a = ___°
b = ___°
c = ___°

Today I scored ___ out of 8.

Week 10 — Day 4

Work out the value of the angle labelled x.

[Example: angles 105°, 95°, 85°, x in a trapezium — answer 75°]

1. 65°, 50°, x → ☐°

2. 140°, 50°, 100°, x → ☐°

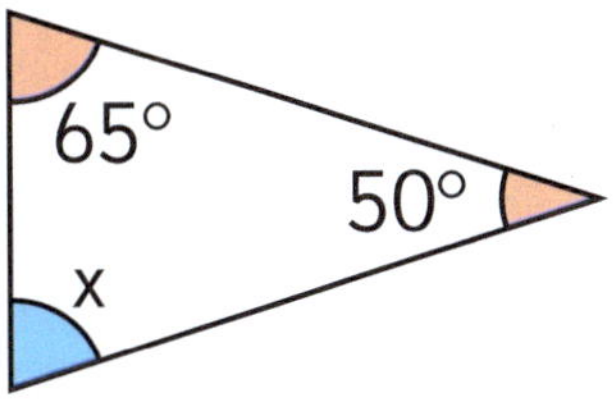

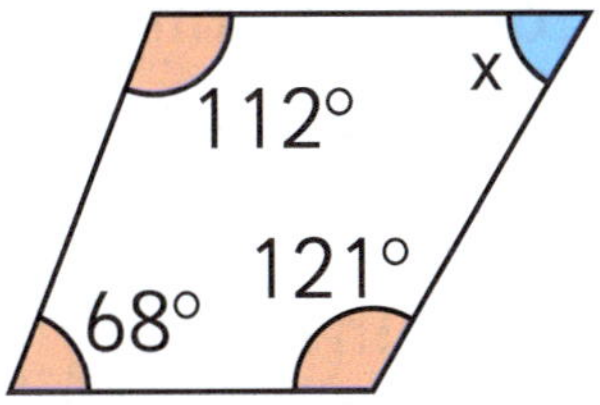

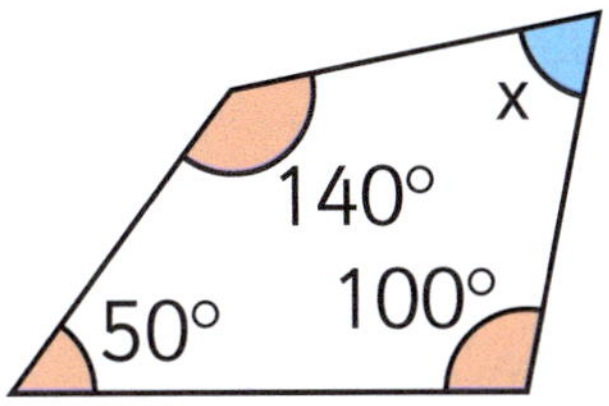

3. Right angle, 53°, x → ☐°

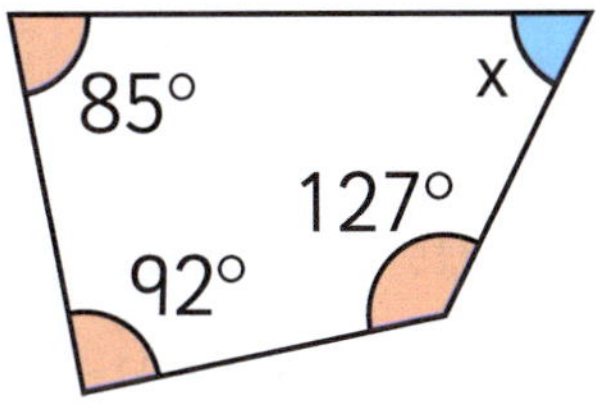

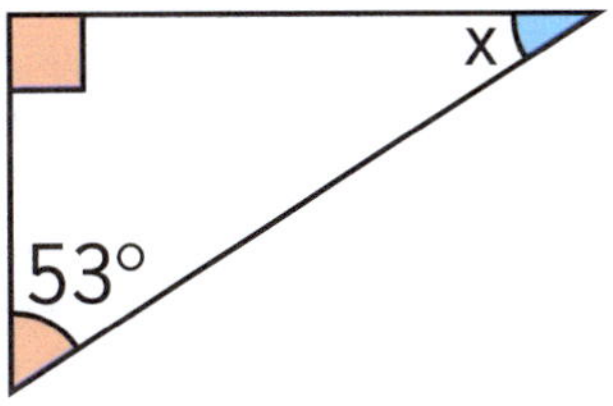

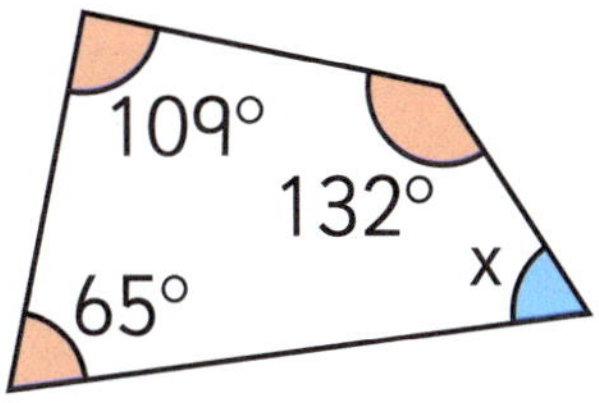

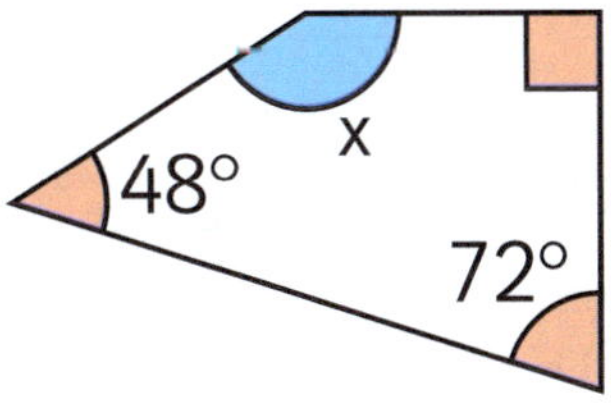

4. 48°, 72°, right angle, x → ☐°

5. 112°, 68°, 121°, x → ☐°

6. 85°, 92°, 127°, x → ☐°

7. 109°, 132°, 65°, x → ☐°

8. 36°, 38°, 29°, x (reflex) → ☐°

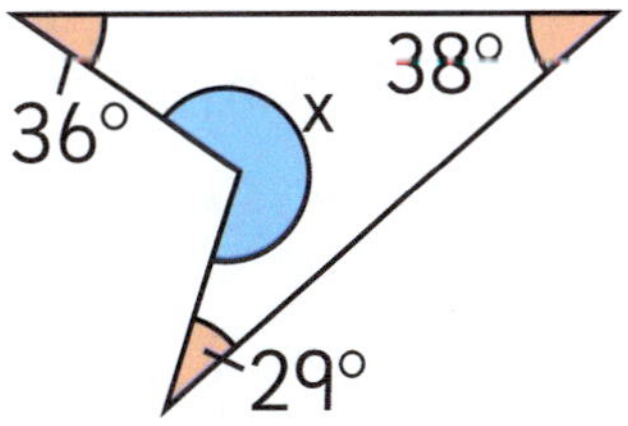

Today I scored ☐ out of 8.

Week 10 — Day 5

Who spent longer at the funfair?

May was at the funfair between 12:05 and 14:15. Diego was at the funfair for 2 hours and 5 minutes.

May

1) Lydia was at the funfair between 14:35 and 15:40. Seb was at the funfair for 1 hour and 10 minutes.

2) Max was at the funfair between 13:30 and 15:00. Joan was at the funfair for 1 hour and 15 minutes.

3) Alice was at the funfair between 10:15 and 12:40. Roy was at the funfair for 2 hours and 45 minutes.

4) Greg was at the funfair between 12:23 and 15:30. Mark was at the funfair for 2 hours and 57 minutes.

5) Ella was at the funfair between 15:20 and 17:08. Jess was at the funfair for 2 hours and 10 minutes.

6) Yara was at the funfair between 11:57 and 16:12. Ada was at the funfair for 4 hours and 8 minutes.

7) Lana was at the funfair between 14:18 and 16:06. Keith was at the funfair for 1 hour and 39 minutes.

8) Ed was at the funfair between 09:13 and 12:05. Nick was at the funfair for 2 hours and 56 minutes.

9) Carol was at the funfair between 14:27 and 17:09. Flora was at the funfair for 2 hours and 45 minutes.

Today I scored ☐ out of 9.

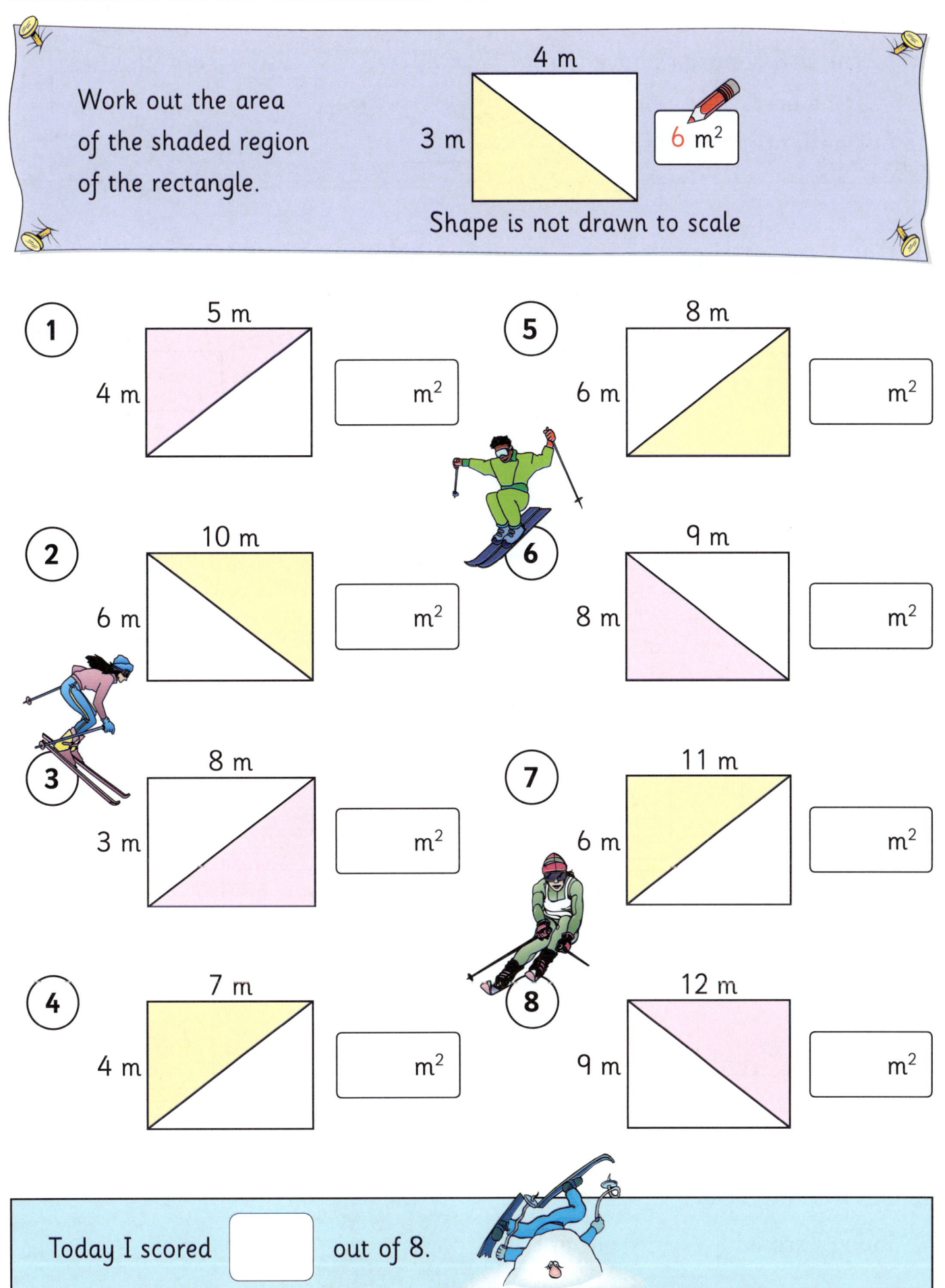

Week 11 — Day 2

The two rectangles have the same area. Work out the length of the side labelled x.

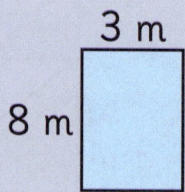
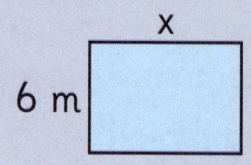
x = **4** m

1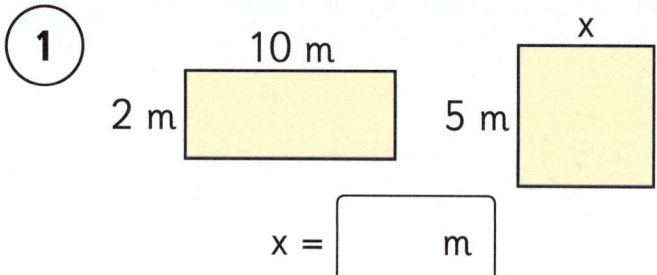
x = ___ m

2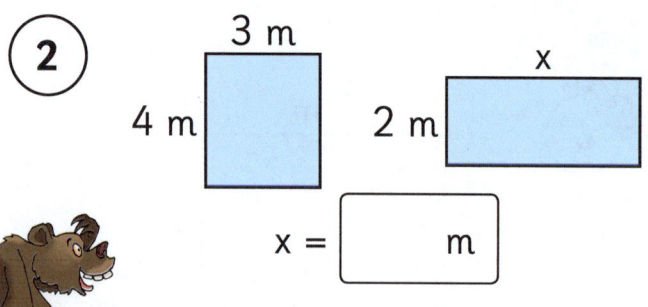
x = ___ m

3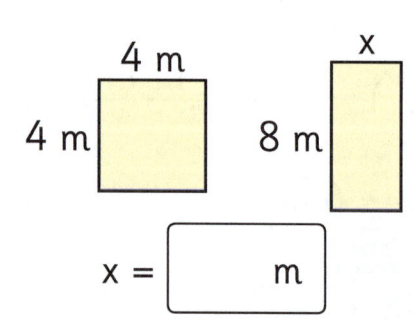
x = ___ m

4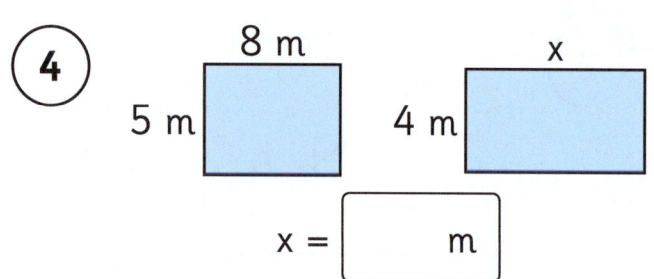
x = ___ m

5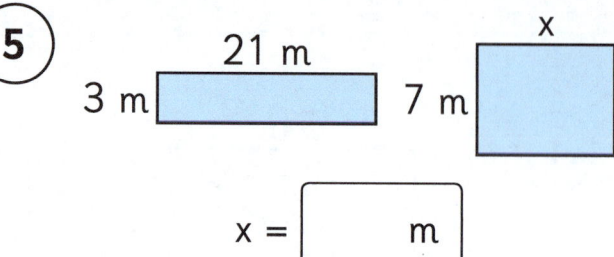
x = ___ m

6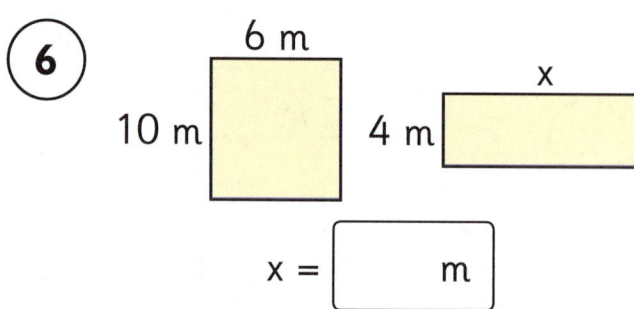
x = ___ m

7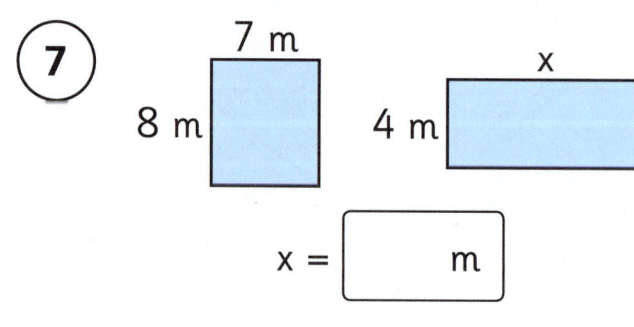
x = ___ m

8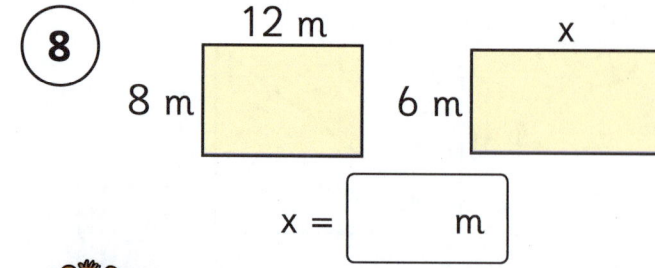
x = ___ m

Today I scored ___ out of 8.

Week 11 — Day 3

Solve the calculation.   12 + 45 ÷ 9 = 17

1) 15 + 5 × 2 =

2) 18 ÷ (4 + 5) =

3) 28 ÷ (5 + 2) =

4) 23 + 9 × 3 =

5) 12 × (8 − 5) =

6) 8 × 11 − 12 =

7) 6 + 7 × 7 =

8) 53 − 21 ÷ 3 =

9) (87 − 6) ÷ 9 =

10) 97 − 121 ÷ 11 =

11) (9 + 3) × 12 =

12) 37 + 9 × 12 =

Today I scored ☐ out of 12.

Week 11 — Day 4

The diagram shows the size of a field. If one cow needs 60 m^2 of land, how many cows can fit in the field?

30 m
20 m

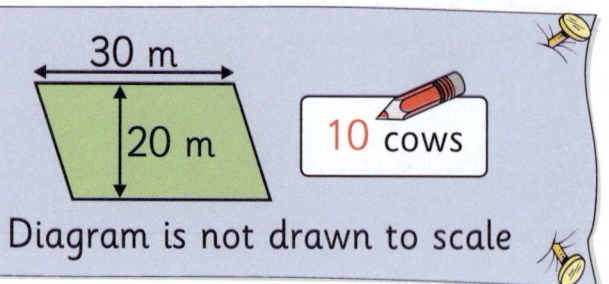

Diagram is not drawn to scale

10 cows

1

100 m
30 m

_____ cows

5

30 m
80 m

_____ cows

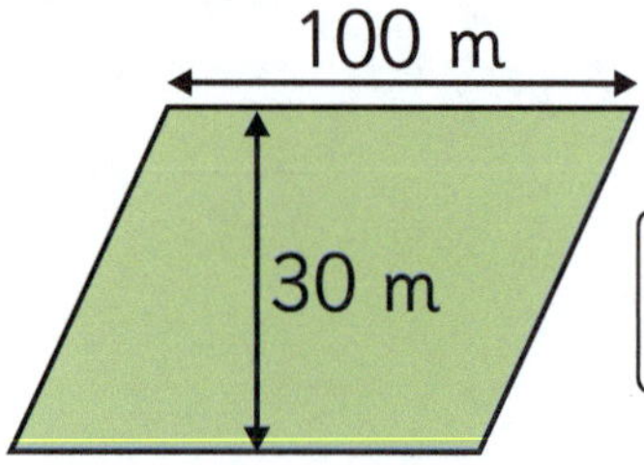

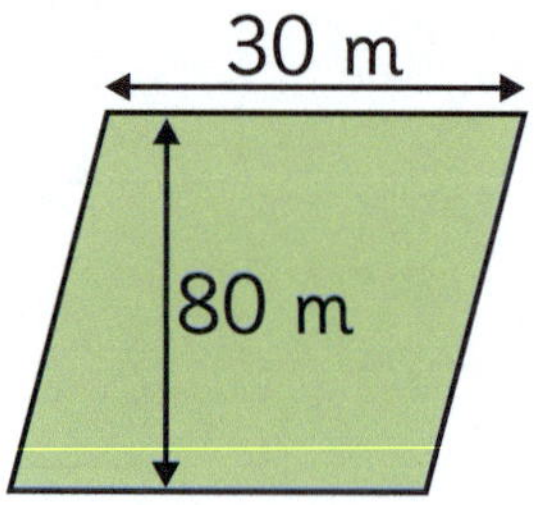

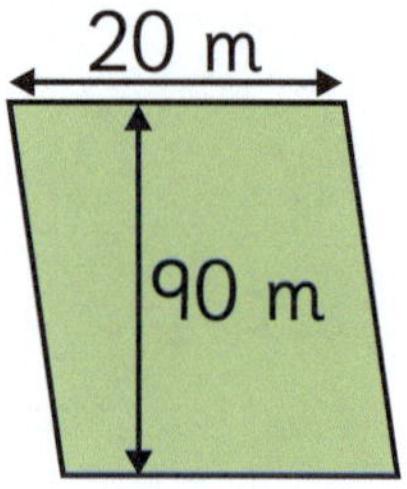

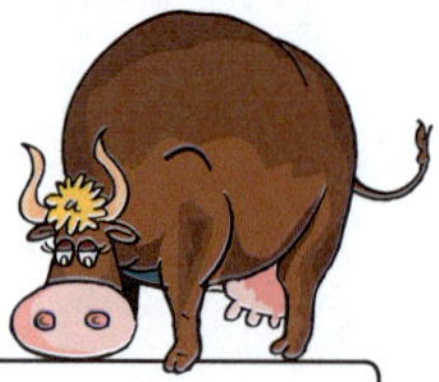

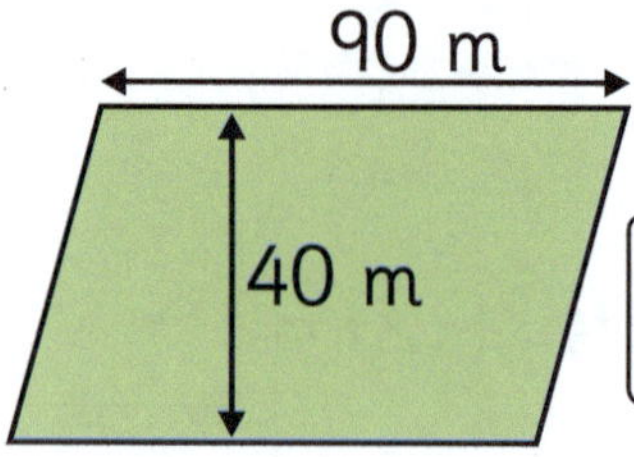

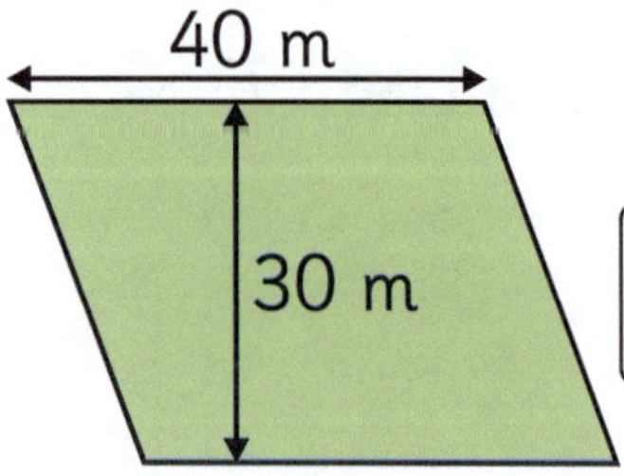

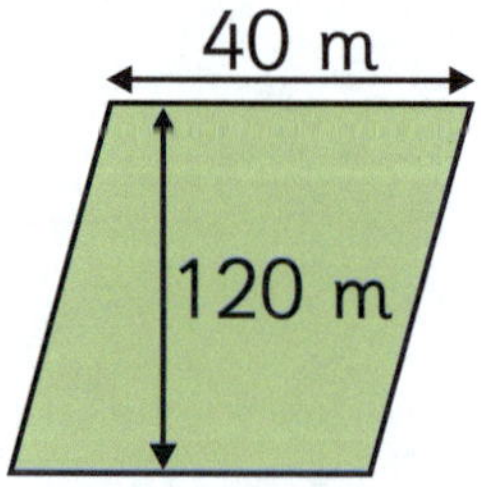

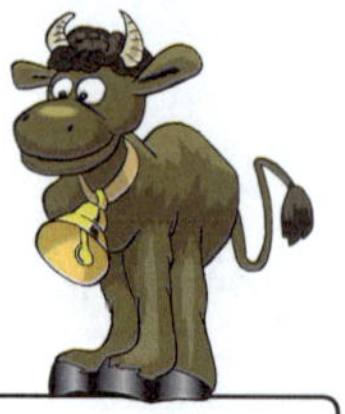

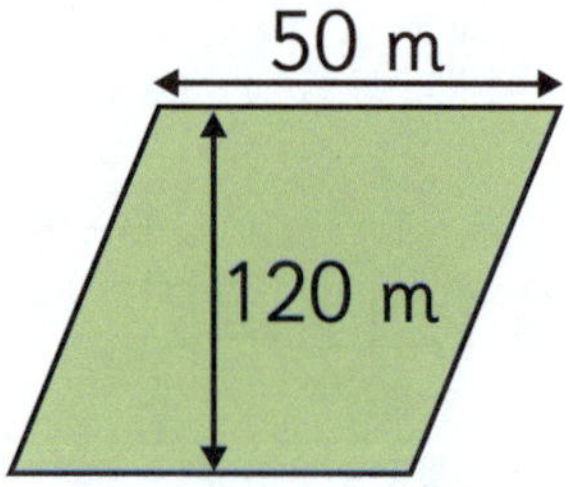

2

20 m
90 m

_____ cows

6

90 m
40 m

_____ cows

3

40 m
30 m

_____ cows

7

40 m
120 m

_____ cows

4

50 m
120 m

_____ cows

8

90 m
80 m

_____ cows

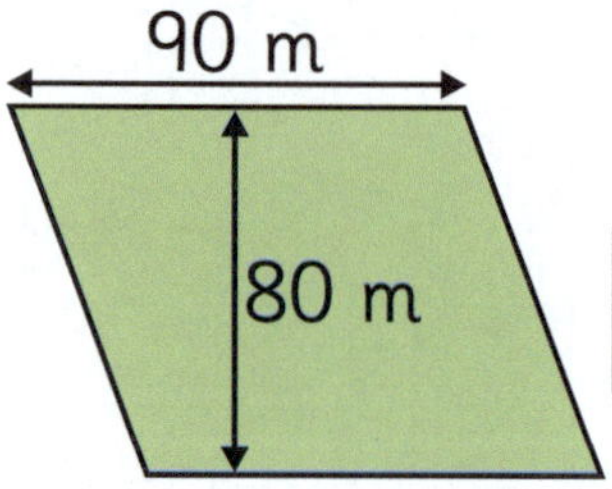

Today I scored _____ out of 8.

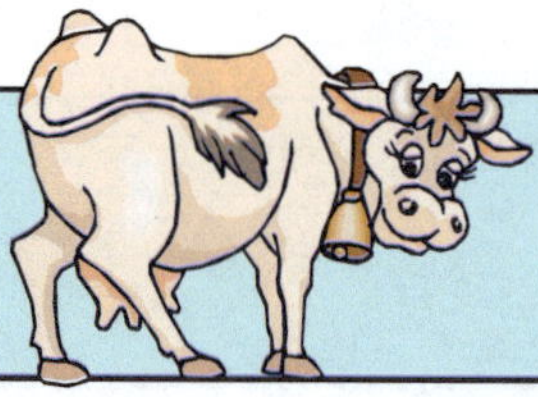

Week 11 — Day 5

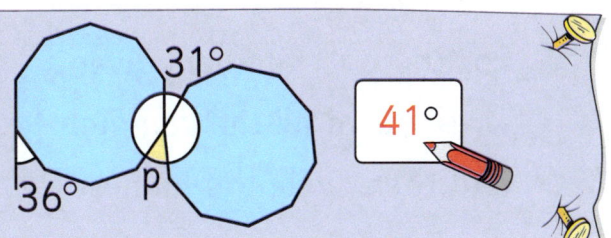

The diagram shows two identical regular polygons or stars. Work out the size of the angle labelled p.

1. p, 140°, 120°

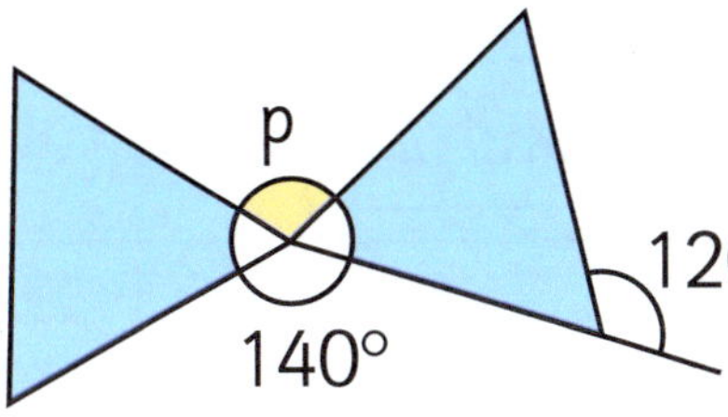

2. p, 165°

3. p, 86°, 60°

4. p, 27°, 40°

5. 58°, p, 45°

6. 30°, p, 39°

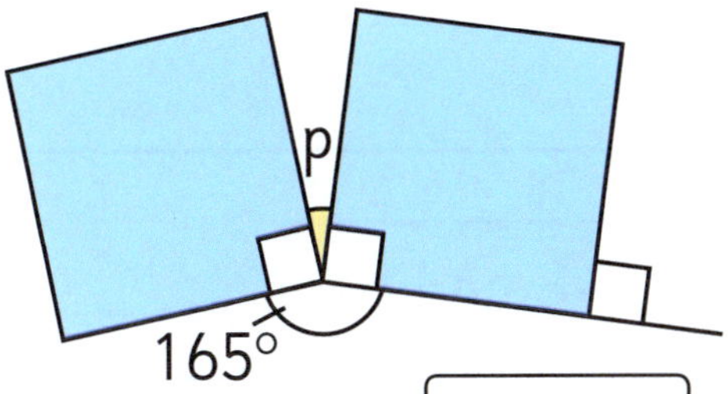

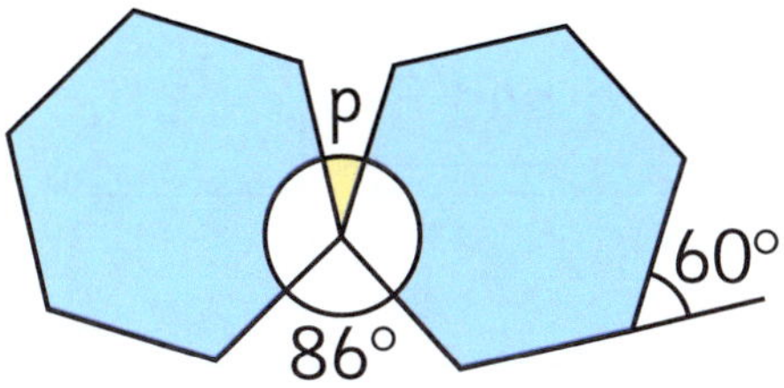

7. 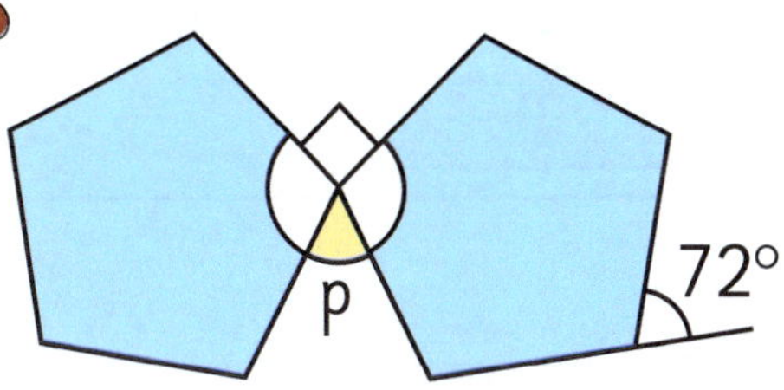 p, 72°

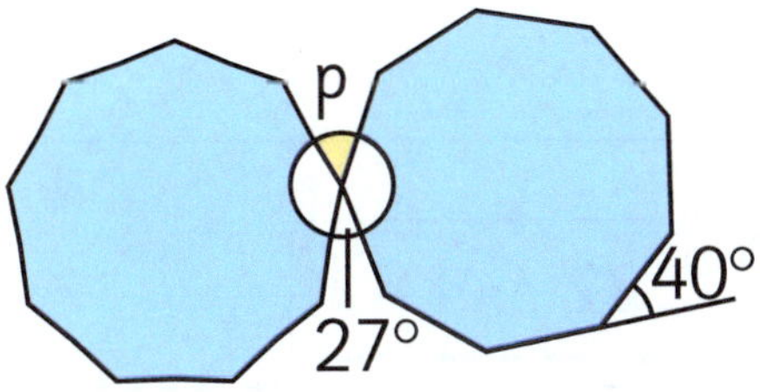

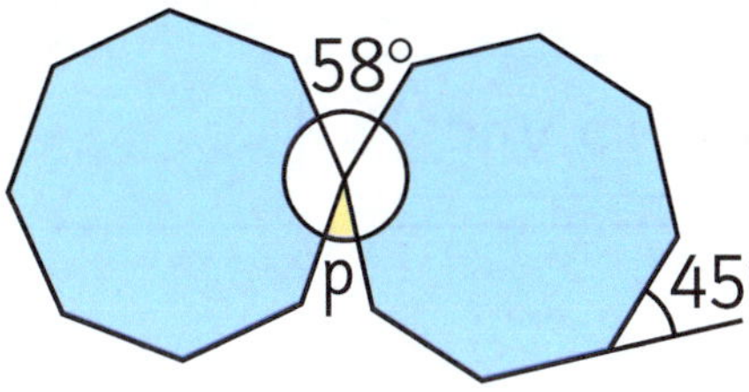

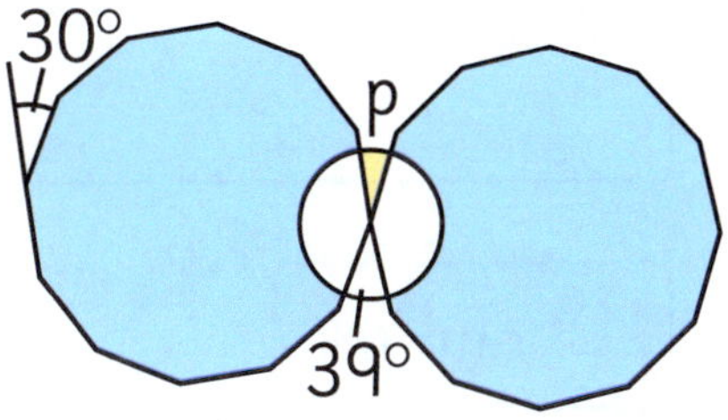

8. 144°, p, 164°

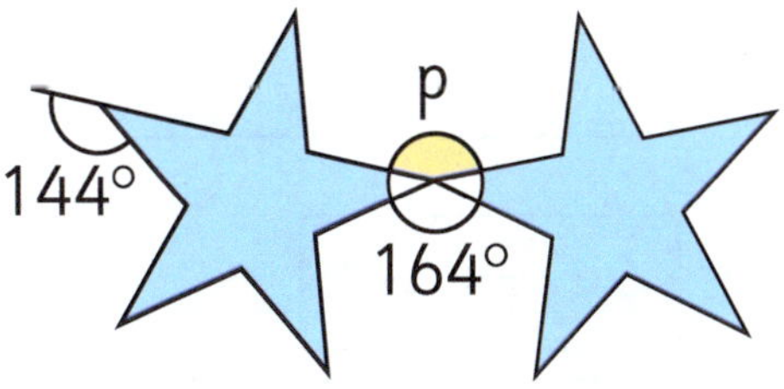

Today I scored ☐ out of 8.

Week 12 — Day 1

For the two numbers given, write down all the common factors and then circle the highest factor.

8 and 12

1, 2, ④

1) 15 and 18

2) 16 and 44

3) 14 and 44

4) 18 and 42

5) 24 and 36

6) 27 and 63

7) 40 and 72

8) 35 and 49

9) 48 and 84

10) 56 and 96

11) 45 and 60

12) 32 and 80

Today I scored ☐ out of 12.

Week 12 — Day 2

Work out the volume of the cuboid.

A cuboid has sides of length 2 m, 5 m and 3 m.

Volume = 30 m³

1) A cuboid has sides of length 4 m, 3 m and 2 m.
Volume = ___ m³

2) A cuboid has sides of length 1 m, 4 m and 6 m.
Volume = ___ m³

3) A cuboid has sides of length 5 m, 9 m and 10 m.
Volume = ___ m³

4) A cuboid has sides of length 2 m, 4 m and 11 m.
Volume = ___ m³

5) A cuboid has sides of length 4 m, 5 m and 4 m.
Volume = ___ m³

6) A cuboid has sides of length 3 m, 3 m and 8 m.
Volume = ___ m³

7) A cuboid has sides of length 6 m, 5 m and 3 m.
Volume = ___ m³

8) A cuboid has sides of length 2 m, 6 m and 8 m.
Volume = ___ m³

9) A cuboid has sides of length 3 m, 4 m and 7 m.
Volume = ___ m³

10) A cuboid has sides of length 3 m, 3 m and 12 m.
Volume = ___ m³

Today I scored ___ out of 10.

Week 12 — Day 3

Use the given values of x and y to solve the calculation.

x = 2, y = 1
x + 2y = 4

1) x = 1, y = 5
2x + y =

2) x = 2, y = 2
x + 3y =

3) x = 10, y = 4
5x + y =

4) x = 7, y = 5
2x − y =

5) x = 30, y = 6
x − 4y =

6) x = 11, y = 7
x + 9y =

7) x = 55, y = 8
x − 6y =

8) x = 3, y = 11
2x + 2y =

9) x = 5, y = 9
4x + 3y =

10) x = 12, y = 8
3x − 2y =

Today I scored ☐ out of 10.

Week 12 — Day 4

Who drove further? Tom drove $\frac{13}{5}$ miles and Priyanka drove $\frac{23}{10}$ miles. → Tom

1) Lee drove $\frac{5}{2}$ miles and Emily drove $\frac{9}{4}$ miles.

2) Tiana drove $\frac{8}{3}$ miles and Amita drove $\frac{15}{6}$ miles.

3) Nicole drove $\frac{11}{4}$ miles and Wayne drove $\frac{25}{8}$ miles.

4) Zola drove $\frac{7}{3}$ miles and Liam drove $\frac{29}{12}$ miles.

5) Cora drove $\frac{12}{5}$ miles and Karina drove $\frac{71}{30}$ miles.

6) George drove $\frac{7}{3}$ miles and Alex drove $\frac{47}{21}$ miles.

7) Rashid drove $\frac{13}{3}$ miles and Leona drove $\frac{31}{9}$ miles.

8) Andy drove $\frac{33}{25}$ miles and Claire drove $\frac{94}{75}$ miles.

9) Ryan drove $\frac{16}{5}$ miles and Tony drove $\frac{51}{15}$ miles.

Today I scored ☐ out of 9.

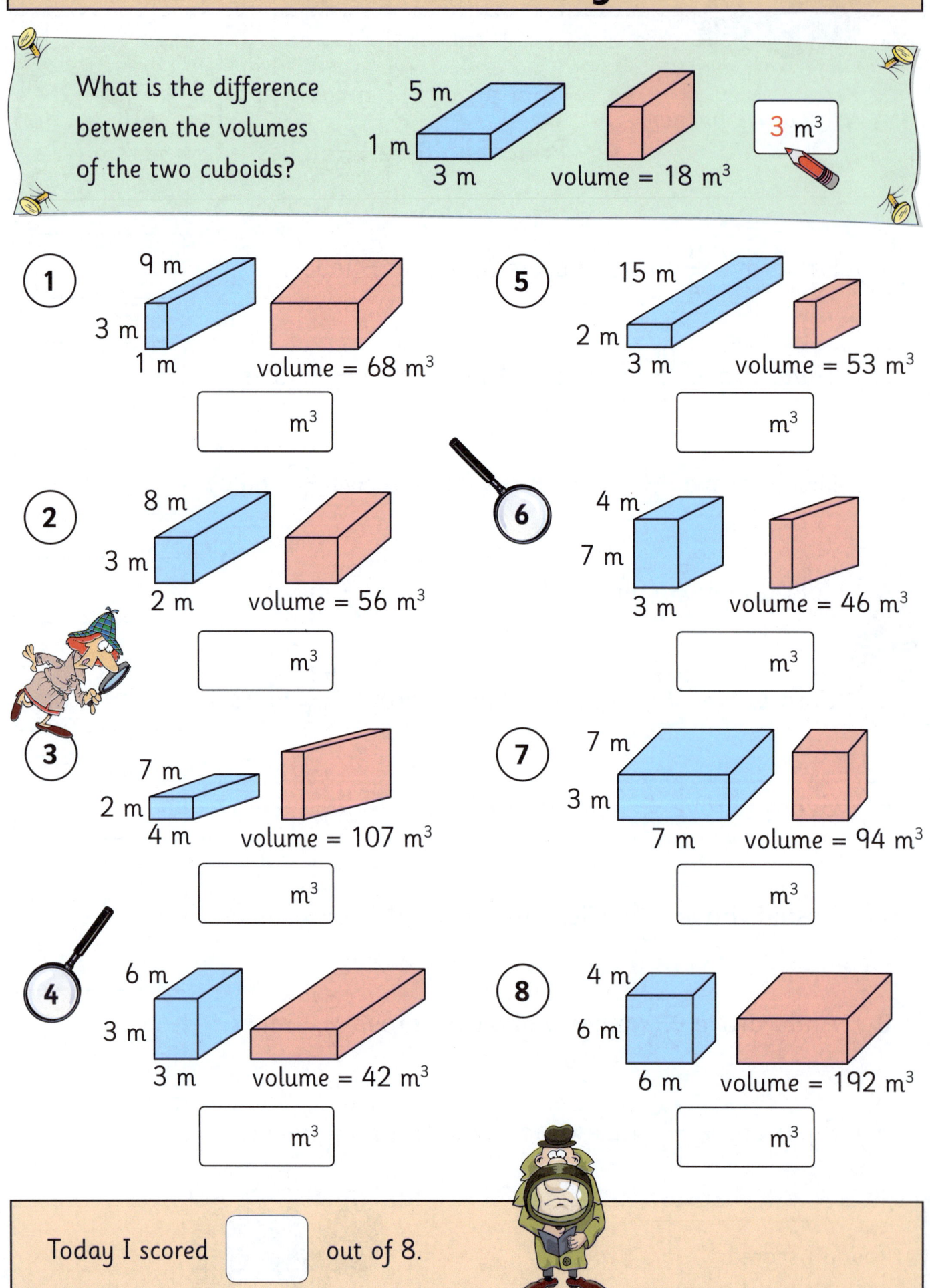

Answers

Week 1 — Day 1
1. 5
2. 37
3. 2
4. 11
5. 7
6. 23
7. 61
8. 67
9. 97
10. 29
11. 53
12. 83

Week 1 — Day 2
1. $3\frac{5}{6}$
2. $7\frac{9}{10}$
3. $3\frac{5}{8}$
4. $7\frac{7}{8}$
5. $8\frac{8}{9}$
6. $5\frac{3}{8}$
7. $1\frac{3}{10}$
8. $9\frac{11}{12}$
9. $3\frac{5}{12}$
10. $7\frac{11}{15}$
11. $2\frac{7}{20}$
12. $8\frac{1}{12}$

Week 1 — Day 3
1. 43 m
2. −10 m
3. 35 m
4. −16 m
5. 39 m
6. −37 m
7. 27 m
8. −65 m
9. 48 m
10. −27 m

Week 1 — Day 4
1. $\frac{1}{12}$
2. $\frac{2}{15}$
3. $\frac{1}{24}$
4. $\frac{1}{9}$
5. $\frac{7}{45}$
6. $\frac{5}{28}$
7. $\frac{3}{32}$
8. $\frac{5}{48}$
9. $\frac{3}{56}$
10. $\frac{2}{21}$
11. $\frac{1}{12}$
12. $\frac{2}{21}$

Week 1 — Day 5
1. $\frac{7}{32}$
2. $\frac{3}{40}$
3. $\frac{3}{8}$
4. $\frac{1}{2}$
5. $\frac{1}{8}$
6. $\frac{8}{15}$
7. $\frac{5}{18}$
8. $\frac{3}{10}$

Week 2 — Day 1
1. 4.48
2. 15.5
3. 9.69
4. 16.04
5. 21.99
6. 20.48
7. 12.52
8. 18.81
9. 42.05
10. 17.56
11. 34.32
12. 57.44

Week 2 — Day 2
1. 60 cm
2. 2.92 m
3. 3800 mm
4. 22 600 cm
5. 71.6 cm
6. 5180 mm
7. 130.1 cm
8. 38.66 m

Week 2 — Day 3
1. £6.40
2. £10.60
3. £9.27
4. £1.26
5. £11.22
6. £12.32
7. £4.66
8. £4.70

Week 2 — Day 4
1. $\frac{6}{10} = 0.6$
2. $\frac{3}{10} = 0.3$
3. $\frac{60}{100} = 0.6$
4. $\frac{70}{100} = 0.7$
5. $\frac{9}{10} = 0.9$
6. $\frac{4}{10} = 0.4$
7. $\frac{7}{10} = 0.7$
8. $\frac{12}{100} = 0.12$
9. $\frac{8}{10} = 0.8$
10. $\frac{84}{100} = 0.84$
11. $\frac{3}{100} = 0.03$
12. $\frac{11}{100} = 0.11$

Week 2 — Day 5
1. 22 minutes
2. 62 minutes
3. 67 minutes
4. 105 minutes
5. 1 h 18 minutes
6. 1 h 36 minutes
7. 1 h 44 minutes
8. 2 h 26 minutes

Week 3 — Day 1
1. 10
2. 10
3. 10
4. 100
5. 1000
6. 1000
7. 10
8. 100
9. 1000
10. 100
11. 1000
12. 1000

Week 3 — Day 2
1. **3** right, **4** down
2. **3** left, **3** down
3. **6** left, **3** up
4. **1** right, **4** down
5. **4** right, **4** down
6. **2** left, **4** down
7. **4** right, **5** up
8. **2** right, **3** down

Week 3 — Day 3
1. Josh
2. Kamala
3. Samuel
4. Louisa
5. Marvin
6. Stefan
7. Kian
8. Raj

Week 3 — Day 4
1. 74% > $\frac{72}{100}$ < 0.76
2. 0.55 > 45% < $\frac{1}{2}$
3. 32% < $\frac{33}{100}$ > 0.31
4. $\frac{3}{4}$ < 76% < 0.77
5. $\frac{9}{10}$ > 0.11 > 10%
6. 0.81 > $\frac{8}{100}$ < 79%
7. $\frac{4}{100}$ > 3% < 0.2
8. 0.04 < $\frac{5}{100}$ < 30%
9. 0.09 = 9% < $\frac{7}{10}$
10. 0.16 > $\frac{3}{50}$ < 60%
11. $\frac{1}{5}$ = 20% > 0.18
12. 0.06 < $\frac{3}{5}$ > 53%

Week 3 — Day 5
1. 20%
2. 50%
3. 71%
4. 30%
5. 23%
6. 17%
7. 11%
8. 38%
9. 40%
10. 46%

Week 4 — Day 1
1. 0, 4
2. 6, 0
3. 8, 0
4. 0, 0
5. 0, 4
6. 0, 1
7. 2, 0
8. 2, 0

Week 4 — Day 2
1. 12, 24, 36
2. 280, 70, 490
3. 36, 240, 48
4. 60, 20, 80
5. 54, 36, 90
6. 560, 42, 84
7. 240, 480, 96
8. 33, 66, 99
9. 360, 108, 72

Week 4 — Day 3
1. 90
2. 70
3. 700
4. 160
5. 540
6. 270
7. 250
8. 330
9. 120
10. 140
11. 320
12. 490

Week 4 — Day 4
1. 20, 5
2. 12, 36
3. 12, 24
4. 40, 30
5. 25, 35
6. 24, 40
7. 32, 56
8. 54, 27

Week 4 — Day 5
1. 240
2. 110
3. 210
4. 120
5. 180
6. 770
7. 840
8. 480

Week 5 — Day 1
1. 9 824 000
2. 7 902 000
3. 400 000
4. 150 000
5. 5 770 000
6. 2 200 000
7. 6 300 000
8. 1 230 000
9. 3 450 000

Week 5 — Day 2
1. £9
2. £2.10
3. £3
4. £4.40
5. £4.80
6. £6.30
7. £6.40
8. £0.75
9. £3.60
10. £2
11. £1.44
12. £10.80

Week 5 — Day 3
1. 5
2. 6
3. 9
4. 8
5. 9
6. 7
7. 4
8. 12

Week 5 — Day 4
1. 5 cm
2. 10 cm
3. 8 cm
4. 7 cm
5. 11 cm
6. 12 cm
7. 20 cm
8. 6 cm

Week 5 — Day 5
1. 30
2. 10
3. 27
4. 60
5. 25
6. 150
7. 36
8. 55
9. 39
10. 42
11. 48
12. 66

Week 6 — Day 1
1. 3 645 109
2. 3 098 678
3. 2 543 156
4. 891 498
5. 1 235 718
6. 7 304 142
7. 9 546 265
8. 5 910 283
9. 9 690 122
10. 4 508 007
11. 6 544 118
12. 2 235 198

Week 6 — Day 2
1. 23, 19
2. 5, 10
3. −17, −20
4. 7, 10
5. 24, 19
6. 7, 13
7. −8, −4
8. 3, 1
9. 11, 32
10. −4, −1
11. 34, 45
12. 50, 14

Week 6 — Day 3
1. 3
   Rule: add $\frac{1}{2}$
2. $4\frac{2}{4}$ (or $4\frac{1}{2}$)
   Rule: subtract $\frac{1}{4}$
3. $4\frac{1}{3}$
   Rule: add $\frac{2}{3}$
4. 5
   Rule: add $\frac{2}{5}$
5. $1\frac{7}{8}$
   Rule: subtract $\frac{2}{8}$ (or $\frac{1}{4}$)
6. $2\frac{3}{7}$
   Rule: subtract $\frac{5}{7}$
7. $5\frac{1}{9}$
   Rule: add $\frac{4}{9}$
8. $4\frac{4}{6}$
   Rule: subtract $\frac{5}{6}$

Week 6 — Day 4
1. 1
2. 17
3. 11
4. 38
5. 20
6. 21
7. −3
8. 45
9. 39
10. 118

Week 6 — Day 5
1. 290 g
2. 175 g
3. 730 g
4. 560 g
5. 88 g
6. 620 g
7. 122 g

Week 7 — Day 1
1. 10
2. 12
3. 5
4. 27
5. 48
6. 10
7. 9
8. 42
9. 12
10. 7
11. 81
12. 132

Week 7 — Day 2
1. $4\frac{4}{6}$ or $4\frac{2}{3}$
2. $2\frac{11}{12}$
3. $6\frac{3}{6}$ or $6\frac{1}{2}$
4. $4\frac{7}{8}$
5. $3\frac{8}{9}$
6. $8\frac{15}{20}$ or $8\frac{3}{4}$
7. $12\frac{7}{8}$
8. $5\frac{9}{12}$ or $5\frac{3}{4}$
9. $10\frac{10}{12}$ or $10\frac{5}{6}$
10. $9\frac{19}{20}$
11. $5\frac{1}{14}$
12. $4\frac{1}{18}$

Week 7 — Day 3
1. $2x + y = 6$
2. $x + y = 6$
3. $2x - y = 1$
4. $x - y = 3$
5. $3x - y = 10$
6. $2x + 2y = 20$
7. $3x - y = 12$
8. $3x + 2y = 16$

Week 7 — Day 4
1. A = 1 B = 3
   A = 2 B = 2
   A = 3 B = 1
2. A = 1 B = 9
   A = 3 B = 3
   A = 9 B = 1
3. A = 1 B = 4
   A = 2 B = 2
   A = 4 B = 1
4. A = 1 B = 6
   A = 2 B = 4
   A = 3 B = 2
5. A = 1 B = 3
   A = 4 B = 2
   A = 7 B = 1
6. A = 2 B = 9
   A = 4 B = 6
   A = 6 B = 3

Week 7 — Day 5
1. $y = 10x$ and $y = 30$
2. $y = 6x$ and $y = 36$
3. $y = 3x + 2$ and $y = 8$
4. $y = 2x - 4$ and $y = 4$
5. $y = 4x + 12$ and $y = 44$
6. $y = 7x + 5$ and $y = 40$
7. $y = 9x + 11$ and $y = 74$
8. $y = 8x - 6$ and $y = 66$
9. $y = 12x - 8$ and $y = 76$

Week 8 — Day 1
1. £2.50
2. £16.50
3. £18.45
4. £4.48
5. £55.99
6. £12.84
7. £16.96
8. £18.45
9. £3.87
10. £25.20
11. £17.50
12. £55.93

Week 8 — Day 2
1. 4125 m
2. 1.956 m
3. 1722 m
4. 243.1 cm
5. 7.563 km
6. 250.3 mm
7. 3.486 km
8. 63.91 mm
9. 391.4 cm
10. 82.35 m
11. 72.34 cm
12. 5091 cm

Week 8 — Day 3
1. =
2. >
3. >
4. =
5. >
6. <
7. >
8. >
9. <
10. <
11. >
12. >

Week 8 — Day 4
1. 10 laps
2. 4 laps
3. 5 laps
4. 9 laps
5. 8 laps
6. 7 laps
7. 14 laps
8. 7 laps
9. 12 laps
10. 11 laps

Week 8 — Day 5
1. 40 miles
2. 38 miles
3. 81 miles
4. 147 miles
5. 475 miles
6. 585 miles
7. 530 miles
8. 1110 miles

Week 9 — Day 1
1. 2500 g
2. 650 g
3. 2400 g
4. 1800 g
5. 82 g
6. 200 g
7. 960 g
8. 840 g
9. 108 g
10. 450 g
11. 246 g
12. 1560 g

Week 9 — Day 2
1. 1800 seconds
2. 3000 seconds
3. 150 minutes
4. 720 minutes
5. 480 hours
6. 4200 seconds
7. 7200 seconds
8. 12 000 seconds
9. 2400 minutes
10. 132 hours

Week 9 — Day 3
1. 4.68 l
2. 3.52 l
3. 2.685 l
4. 4.36 l
5. 3.6 l
6. 2.21 l
7. 3.789 l
8. 4.187 l
9. 4.299 l
10. 4.095 l

Week 9 — Day 4
1. 40 weeks
2. 1 week
3. 9 weeks
4. 100 weeks
5. 20 weeks
6. 6 weeks
7. 50 weeks
8. 12 weeks

Week 9 — Day 5
1. 260 g
2. 1100 g
3. 120 g
4. 2020 g
5. 470 g
6. 1335 g
7. 1775 g
8. 3010 g

Week 10 — Day 1

1. $\frac{40}{12}$
2. $\frac{28}{35}$
3. $\frac{11}{4}$
4. $\frac{63}{42}$
5. $\frac{72}{81}$
6. $\frac{72}{84}$
7. $\frac{21}{6}$
8. $\frac{12}{9}$
9. $\frac{20}{8}$
10. $\frac{18}{75}$
11. $\frac{2}{10}$
12. $\frac{24}{9}$

Week 10 — Day 2

1. $\frac{1}{8}$
2. $\frac{3}{50}$
3. $\frac{1}{6}$
4. $\frac{2}{9}$
5. $\frac{1}{5}$
6. $\frac{7}{64}$
7. $\frac{2}{21}$
8. $\frac{5}{81}$
9. $\frac{1}{22}$
10. $\frac{2}{63}$
11. $\frac{1}{32}$
12. $\frac{1}{27}$

Week 10 — Day 3

1. a = 120°, b = 60°, c = 120°
2. a = 30°, b = 150°, c = 30°
3. a = 94°, b = 86°, c = 94°
4. a = 11°, b = 169°, c = 11°
5. a = 67°, b = 113°, c = 67°
6. a = 102°, b = 78°, c = 102°
7. a = 144°, b = 36°, c = 144°
8. a = 139°, b = 41°, c = 139°

Week 10 — Day 4

1. 65°
2. 70°
3. 37°
4. 150°
5. 59°
6. 56°
7. 54°
8. 257°

Week 10 — Day 5

1. Seb
2. Max
3. Roy
4. Greg
5. Jess
6. Yara
7. Lana
8. Nick
9. Flora

Week 11 — Day 1

1. 10 m²
2. 30 m²
3. 12 m²
4. 14 m²
5. 24 m²
6. 36 m²
7. 33 m²
8. 54 m²

Week 11 — Day 2

1. 4 m
2. 6 m
3. 2 m
4. 10 m
5. 9 m
6. 15 m
7. 14 m
8. 16 m

Week 11 — Day 3

1. 25
2. 2
3. 4
4. 50
5. 36
6. 76
7. 55
8. 46
9. 9
10. 86
11. 144
12. 145

Week 11 — Day 4

1. 50 cows
2. 30 cows
3. 20 cows
4. 100 cows
5. 40 cows
6. 60 cows
7. 80 cows
8. 120 cows

Week 11 — Day 5

1. 100°
2. 15°
3. 34°
4. 53°
5. 32°
6. 21°
7. 54°
8. 124°

Week 12 — Day 1

1. 1, ③
2. 1, 2, ④
3. 1, ②
4. 1, 2, 3, ⑥
5. 1, 2, 3, 4, 6, ⑫
6. 1, 3, ⑨
7. 1, 2, 4, ⑧
8. 1, ⑦
9. 1, 2, 3, 4, 6, ⑫
10. 1, 2, 4, ⑧
11. 1, 3, 5, ⑮
12. 1, 2, 4, 8, ⑯

Week 12 — Day 2

1. 24 m³
2. 24 m³
3. 450 m³
4. 88 m³
5. 80 m³
6. 72 m³
7. 90 m³
8. 96 m³
9. 84 m³
10. 108 m³

Week 12 — Day 3

1. 7
2. 8
3. 54
4. 9
5. 6
6. 74
7. 7
8. 28
9. 47
10. 20

Week 12 — Day 4

1. Lee
2. Tiana
3. Wayne
4. Liam
5. Cora
6. George
7. Rashid
8. Andy
9. Tony

Week 12 — Day 5

1. 41 m³
2. 8 m³
3. 51 m³
4. 12 m³
5. 37 m³
6. 38 m³
7. 53 m³
8. 48 m³